Contents

The Scout District

The Scout County

The Policy, Organisation and Rules of The Scout Association

£1:13

Part One
Organisation

The Scout Association
Baden–Powell House
Queen's Gate
London SW7 5JS

Copyright © 1977
The Scout Association
ISBN 0 85165 128 3

**First Edition
March 1977
Fourth Printing
November 1983**

Designed by: Flavia Malim

Printed in Great Britain by
Eyre & Spottiswoode Ltd at Grosvenor Press,
Portsmouth

National

Introduction

As the recognised national Association in the United Kingdom, The Scout Association is a member of the World Scout Conference. Its own organisation exists by the authority of a Royal Charter, granted by King George V in 1912 and supplemented by further Charters granted by King George VI and Queen Elizabeth II. These Charters give authority to the Bye Laws of the Association, which are approved by Her Majesty's Privy Council. The Bye Laws, in turn, authorise the making of rules for the regulation of the Association's affairs. These have become known as *'Policy, Organisation and Rules'* or, more usually, *'P.O.R.'* and they establish the pattern of the organisation, define its training and provide the skeleton, without which Scouting could not function mechanically, but which is by no means the whole being of the Association.

The Founder called the first set of rules 'Rules for Playing the Game of Scouting', stressing at the outset that it was the practice of good Scouting that was important and not any ponderous collection of regulations which might be interpreted as hampering the man on the spot. Nothing in the Association's attitude has changed over the years. Although they are all integral parts of the Scout Movement every Scout Group is separately registered and has its own individuality. Because of this their structure, operation and standards must be organised and run along common, clearly defined lines. Even so, Scouting is still a game and if other games have rules so that the players know who wins, Scouting needs its rules so that the game can be played well.

Preface

In order to overcome problems that were evident in previous editions of *Policy, Organisation and Rules,* the rules of the Association are here presented in a revised order and the wording of the entire text has been brought into a single style. The Directory, which appears in both Parts, has been greatly expanded to make it easier to find references quickly.

Rules are numbered here in the same way as in Part Two. References are given as *Rule I, 2 ii,* meaning Rule 2 ii in Part One, or *II, 5 iii (a),* meaning Rule 5 iii (a), in Part Two. Reference to earlier rules in this Part are given as *'See Rule 4 iii above'* and later rules are referred to as *'See Rule I, 5 iii'.*

Keeping your copy up to date

In order to facilitate the process of amendment, a new system has been introduced. Space is provided by a margin on each page in which the reader should put a mark, together with a note of the number of the page on which the amendment appears. This will refer to one of the numbered blank pages which are to be found at the end of the book. The text of amendments will be given, from time to time, in *Headquarters Notices* in SCOUTING Magazine. They will be printed to a style and layout to conform with this book and should be cut out and pasted in this final section. Reprints of this edition will contain asterisks against amended rules with page references indicating the number of the page on which the text of the amendment will be printed. In new editions, rules will be brought up to date and the pages at the end will again appear blank.

Scotland

Under the Constitution for Scotland, the affairs of The Scout Association in Scotland are under the charge of The Scottish Council, which is the National Council established under *Rule I, 75 ii*, with a Committee for the management of its business.

Under the authority of the Headquarters of The Scout Association, Scottish Headquarters is the body responsible for matters of programme, training and administration in Scotland and is the channel for all communications with the Headquarters of the Association unless a specific invitation has been made for direct communication.

Scotland has separate government, legal and educational systems and a different system of two tier local government in Districts and Regions. Certain rules must therefore be interpreted as applying to Scotland with appropriate variations in their wording, particularly:

(a) references to Scout Counties should be read as *Areas* when related to Scotland;

(b) the rules concerning title deeds and leases of property *(Rule I, 29)* do not apply to Scotland;

(c) charitable status is granted in Scotland by the Inland Revenue and not under the Charities Act, 1960 *(See Rule I, 28 iii)*;

(d) for details of the Quest emblem, awarded in Scotland and Northern Ireland, see the Preface to Part Two.

Northern Ireland

Under the Constitution for Northern Ireland, the affairs of The Scout Association in Northern Ireland are under the charge of the Northern Ireland Scout Council, which is the National Council established under *Rule I, 75 ii*, with a Committee for the management of its business.

Under the authority of the Headquarters of The Scout Association, Northern Ireland Headquarters is the body responsible for matters of programme, training and administration in Northern Ireland and is the channel for all communications with the Headquarters of the Association unless a specific invitation has been made for direct communication.

Northern Ireland has separate government, legal and educational systems and a different system of two tier local government in Districts and Education and Library Boards. Certain rules must therefore be interpreted as applying to Northern Ireland with appropriate variations in their wording, particularly:

(a) charitable status is granted in Northern Ireland by the Inland Revenue and not under the Charities Act, 1960;

(b) for details of the Quest emblem, awarded in Northern Ireland and Scotland, see the Preface to Part Two.

Wales

While there is a National Council – the Welsh Scout Council – for Wales, the Headquarters of The Scout Association undertakes all the functions of the National Headquarters in respect of both England and Wales.

Rule 1   Aim and Method

The Aim of The Scout Association is to encourage the physical, mental and spiritual development of young people so that they may take a constructive place in society. The Method of achieving the Aim of the Association is by providing an enjoyable and attractive scheme of progressive training, based on the Scout Promise and Law and guided by adult leadership.

Rule 2   Promise and Law

Rule 2 i   The Scout Promise and Law

The Scout Promise and Law are as follows:

Promise

On my honour, I promise that I will do my best
to do my duty to God and to the Queen,
to help other people
and to keep the Scout Law.

Law

1. A Scout is to be trusted.
2. A Scout is loyal.
3. A Scout is friendly and considerate.
4. A Scout is a brother to all Scouts.
5. A Scout has courage in all difficulties.
6. A Scout makes good use of his time and is careful of possessions and property.
7. A Scout has respect for himself and for others.

Rule 2 ii   The Cub Scout Promise and Law

The Cub Scout Promise and Law are as follows:

Promise

I promise that I will do my best
to do my duty to God and to the Queen,
to help other people
and to keep the Cub Scout Law.

Law
A Cub Scout always does his best,
thinks of others before himself
and does a good turn every day.

Rule 2 iii   The Outlander Promise

Since Scouting is available to the adherents of all religions, it must take account of different religious obligations. Similarly, foreign residents, who may become Members of the Association (*See Rule I, 3 i*), owe allegiance to their own head of State. To meet these circumstances, there are different forms of the Scout Promise that can be made, allowing for the individual's obligations and upholding the essential spirit of the Promise. A variation of the basic form permitted under this rule is known as an Outlander Promise, details of which may be obtained from Headquarters.

Rule 3   Membership

Rule 3 i   Qualifications for Membership

British subjects and, with the approval of the appropriate Commissioner, foreign residents in the United Kingdom, who are prepared to follow the Association's principles by making the Scout Promise may become Members of The Scout Association, subject to the provisions of these rules.

*Sub-Rule 3 ii amended. See page 134.

Rule 3 ii   Rights and Conditions of Membership

Members of the Association may:
□ wear the approved uniform of the Association until reaching the age of sixty-five years;
□ wear the World Membership Badge;
Adult Members who do not hold appointments

will receive the appropriate Membership Card on payment of the annual Membership Subscription.

Rule 3 iii   Age Limits

(a) The minimum age limit for Membership of the Association is eight years. There is no maximum age limit for Membership as such, but certain appointments are subject to both minimum and maximum age limits as stated in these rules.

(b) In cases where Membership is conferred by the granting of an appointment, it will cease upon the retirement of the holder due to his reaching the maximum age limit for the appointment.

Rule 3 iv   Acquisition of Membership

Membership of the Association may be acquired by making the Promise in an Investiture ceremony, in the case of Cub Scouts, Scouts and Venture Scouts and by:

□ appointment, in the case of the holders of all Leader Warrants, of Instructors, Administrators and Advisers and in the case of Honorary Scouters *(See Note below)*;

□ annual registration and payment of the annual Membership Subscription, in the case of Deep Sea Scouts;

□ payment of the annual Membership Subscription in all other cases.

Note: Honorary Scouters

The title *Honorary Scouter* may be conferred by the Headquarters of the Association on a Warrant holder who retires and who has completed at least ten years of outstanding warranted service. Recommendations for the appointment of Honorary Scouters are made by District Commissioners on Form W or, in the case of Commissioners other than County Commissioners, by County Commissioners on Form X. Headquarters will endorse the cancelled Warrant of the Honorary Scouter accordingly. This honorary appointment does not carry any title other than that of Honorary Scouter and lapses if a further warranted appointment is made.

Rule 3 v   Associate Membership of the Association – Qualifications

Members of Group Councils and of the District Scout Fellowship who do not wish to make the Scout Promise may become Associate Members of the Association.

Rule 3 vi   Rights and Conditions of Associate Membership

Associate Members of the Association may:
□ wear the Associate's lapel badge;
□ receive the appropriate Membership Card on payment of the annual Membership Subscription.

Rule 3 vii   Acquisition of Associate Membership

Associate Membership is acquired on joining the District Scout Fellowship (*See Rule I, 51*) or, in the case of members of a Group Council, through application to the District Secretary, and, in both cases, by paying the annual Membership Subscription.

*New sub-Rule 3 viii. See page 134. Present sub-Rule 3 viii now renumbered as 3 xi.

Rule 3 viii   Termination of Membership

(a) Notwithstanding any other means provided by these rules, the Membership of any Member of the Association may be terminated by a resolution of the Committee of the Council of the Association. The Committee shall be under no obligation to state its reasons for making such a resolution.

(b) Membership may be terminated by:

☐ in the case of Cub Scouts, Scouts and Venture Scouts, leaving their Scout unit or dismissal;

☐ in the case of holders of all appointments, relinquishing the appointment, unless Membership has been acquired by any means other than the granting of the appointment;

☐ in the case of Deep Sea Scouts, failing to register or to pay the annual Membership Subscription;

☐ the cancellation of a Warrant following suspension;

☐ failure to pay the annual Membership Subscription.

*New sub-Rule 3 ix. See page 134. Present sub-Rule 3 ix now renumbered as 3 xii.

Rule 3 ix   Termination of Associate Membership

Associate Membership of the Association may be terminated:

(a) in accordance with *Rule 3 viii (a) above*;

(b) by ceasing to be a member of a District Scout Fellowship or Group Council

(c) by failing to pay the annual Membership Subscription.

*New sub-Rule 3 x. See page 135. Present sub-Rule 3 x now renumbered as 3 xiv.

Rule 3 x   Suspension of Membership and Associate Membership

(a) If it appears necessary to terminate the Membership of a Member or of an Associate Member of the Association subject to investigation, or if such a Member does not acquiesce when informed that a recommendation is to made for the cancellation of such membership, or if it appears desirable for any other reason, such Membership may be suspended by the appropriate authority, viz:

in the case of:

- County Commissioners, by the National Headquarters;
- other Commissioners, by the County Commissioner;
- County and District Administrators and Advisers, by the County Commissioner;
- District and Group Scouters, Instructors, Group Administrators, Advisers, Members and Associate Members, by the District Commissioner.

(b) During a suspension under this rule, any Warrant or Certificate of Appointment must be surrendered to the suspending authority. The suspended Member or Associate Member must refrain from participating in any activity connected with the Association and must not wear uniform or badges. Any appointment held will be regarded as vacant.

(c) A District Commissioner who wishes to suspend any Member or Associate Member of the Association must report the matter with full details to the County Commissioner. He must also notify:

- the County Secretary,
- the District Secretary,
- the Sponsoring Authority (*See Rule I, 4 ii (c)*) if any,
- his National Headquarters,
- the Field Commissioner (if any).

(d) The County Commissioner must be satisfied that suspension is necessary and that the matter cannot be resolved under the provision of any rule or practice of the Association. If he is so satisfied, he will direct the County Secretary to convene a Committee of Inquiry, which will be conducted in accordance with *Standing Orders for the Conduct of Committees of Inquiry following Suspension*, copies of which can be obtained from the National Headquarters.

(e) A County Commissioner who suspends any Member or Associate Member must immediately report the matter with full details to his National Headquarters, who will give instructions for the convening and conduct of a Committee of Inquiry.

(f) The procedures detailed in this rule must not be applied to Cub Scouts, Scouts or Venture Scouts, whose dismissal must be in accordance with *Rule I, 9*.

*New
sub-Rule
3 xiii.
See page 135.

The Scout Group

Rule 4 Types of Scout Group

Rule 4 i

Scout Groups may be registered in one of the following categories:

(a) The Open Scout Group, not related to any other organisation and having a policy of unrestricted recruitment;

(b) The Sponsored (Open) Group, registered by organisations approved for this purpose by the Headquarters of the Association, including those listed below, and having a policy of unrestricted recruitment:

- churches,
- the Salvation Army,
- universities, colleges and schools,
- community service clubs (e.g. Rotary, Lions, etc.),
- industrial or commercial firms,
- local Education Authorities,
- hospitals and institutions,
- formations of Her Majesty's Forces (*See Rule I, 4 ii*).

(c) The Sponsored (Closed) Group, registered by organisations approved for this purpose as in *Rule 4 i (b) above,* and having a policy of restricted recruitment as determined by the Sponsoring Authority *(See Rule I, 4 iii).*

Rule 4 ii The Sponsored (Open) Group

Scout Groups registered as Sponsored (Open) Groups have a policy of unrestricted recruitment.

*Sub-Rule
4 ii (a)
amended.
See page 142.

(a) The person or committee appointed by the organisation which sponsors the Group to exercise its functions in relation to the Group is known as the *Sponsoring Authority*. In Sponsored Groups registered by churches of the Church of England or the Church in Wales, the incumbent is the Sponsoring Authority. He may appoint to act jointly with him or in his place as circumstances may warrant either the Church Wardens or the Parochial Church Council. The District Commissioner must be informed if such an appointment is made.

(b) Responsibilities of the Sponsoring Authority

On receipt of an application for the registration of a Sponsored (Open) Group, the District Commissioner must satisfy himself that the Sponsoring Authority is prepared to discharge the following responsibilities:

□ to accept the policy of the Association as defined in these rules, his attention being drawn to the Association's requirements as to minimum standards for Scout Groups and for Sections within Groups as defined in *Rule I, 7;*

□ to encourage the development of Scouting in the Group and to give the fullest possible encouragement and assistance to the Group Scout Leader in carrying out his duties;

□ to provide suitable accommodation for the Group and opportunities for training;

□ to maintain the continuity of leadership and to approve Scouters for appointment subject to the provisions of *Rule I, 10;*

□ to provide financial support or to ensure that the Group is able to acquire funds adequate to the fulfilment of its training programme;

□ to prepare an agreement in regard to property and equipment to be adhered to by the Sponsoring Authority and the Group and to be recorded annually by the District Secret-

★Addition to
sub-Rule
4 ii (b).
See page 142.

ary. The form of agreement at Appendix A is recommended for this purpose.

(c) Rights of the Sponsoring Authority

The Sponsoring Authority may nominate a representative on the Group Executive Committee. He has the right of consultation with the District Commissioner who must take all reasonable steps to ascertain the Authority's views before taking decisions on matters affecting the Group, particularly:

□ Group registration or recognition of a Section *(See Rule I, 5)*;

□ the amalgamation of the Group with another *(See Rule I, 4 v (d))*;

□ matters affecting the Warrants of Scouters in the Group, specifically signifying his approval of candidates for Warrants *(See Rule I, 10)*;

□ the suspension of any Scouter, unless, in the opinion of the District Commissioner, this is a matter of such urgency that there is insufficient time for such consultation *(See Rule 3 x (c) above)*;

□ an appeal by a Cub Scout, Scout or Venture Scout against dismissal *(See Rule I, 9)*.

★Delete sub-
Rule 4 ii (d).

(d) Responsibilities of Sponsoring Authorities within the Training Programme

If a Sponsored (Open) Group is sponsored by a church or religious body, the Sponsoring Authority is responsible for the spiritual development of those Cub Scouts, Scouts and Venture Scouts who belong to the religion or denomination of the religious body. All other aspects of Scout training remain the responsibility and province of the Group Scout Leader.

★Present sub-
Rule 4 ii (e)
now
renumbered
as 4 ii (d).

(e) Disputes

In the event of a dispute between the Sponsoring Authority and the Group Scout Leader, the matter must be referred to the District Commissioner. Both the Sponsoring Authority and the Group Scout Leader must be given reasonable opportunity to state their cases. *(See also Rule I, 31.)*

Rule 4 iii   Sponsored (Closed) Groups

Groups registered as Sponsored (Closed) Groups have a policy of restricted recruitment as the Sponsoring Authority defines.

(a) No restriction on recruitment may be made which contravenes the provisions of any Statute or enactment.

(b) *Rule 4 ii (a), (b) and (c) above* apply to Sponsored (Closed) Groups in exactly the same way as they apply to Sponsored (Open) Groups.

*Delete sub-Rule 4 iii (c).

(c) Rights of the Sponsoring Authority

If the Sponsoring Authority of a Sponsored (Closed) Group which is sponsored by a church informs the District Commissioner that he is dissatisfied with a Scouter on the grounds that he is not fulfilling his religious duties either by example or precept, the District Commissioner must give effect to these views and take appropriate action.

*Delete sub-Rule 4 iii (d).

(d) Responsibilities of Sponsoring Authorities within the Training Programme

If a Sponsored (Closed) Group is made up of members of one religious body, the Sponsoring Authority is responsible for the spiritual development of the Cub Scouts, Scouts and Venture Scouts. All other aspects of Scout training remain the responsibility and province of the Group Scout Leader.

Rule 4 iv   University, College and School Groups

(a) Groups may be registered by universities, colleges or schools, either as Sponsored (Open) Groups or as Sponsored (Closed) Groups. In such Sponsored (Open) Groups, membership will be open to both pupils or students and to young people who do not attend the university, college or school. In Sponsored (Closed) Groups registered by these bodies, membership will be restricted to present and former pupils or students.

(b) The membership of Groups registered by these bodies must be voluntary.

(c) The District Commissioner must be satisfied that a Head Teacher of a school is prepared, as the Sponsoring Authority, to discharge those responsibilities defined in *Rule 4 ii (b) above*. The Group Scout Leader and the Head Teacher may seek relaxation of some of the provisions of this rule, if exceptional circumstances warrant it, by applying to the District Commissioner.

Rule 4 v Agreements with Sponsoring Authorities

(a) A formal agreement between the District Commissioner and the Sponsoring Authority must be prepared at the time of the initial registration *(See Rule I, 5)* of a Sponsored Group and must specify the responsibilities of the Sponsoring Authority, including those listed in *Rule 4 ii (b) above*. In the case of Sponsored (Closed) Groups, such Sponsorship Agreements must also include a definition of the qualification for membership of the Group in accordance with *Rule 4 iii* and *4 iii (a) above*.

(b) The agreement should follow the form shown at Appendix B, with modification only to suit the particular requirements of the different categories of Group.

*Sub-Rule 4 v (c) amended. See page 142.

(c) The agreement must be reviewed by both parties at least every five years but may be reviewed at any time at the request of either party. It must also be reviewed in the event of a change of Sponsoring Authority.

(d) Amalgamation of Sponsored Groups

It is essential that no steps be taken towards the amalgamation of a Sponsored Group with another Group without the full consent of the Sponsoring Authority. If a Sponsored Group meets the minimum standards for Scout Groups, as defined in *Rule 1, 7,* and the Sponsoring Authority does not desire amalgamation with another Group, his wishes are to be respected. Under no circumstances must amalgamation be effected against the wishes of a Sponsoring Authority.

Rule 5

The Formation and Registration of Scout Groups

Rule 5 i

No steps may be taken towards the formation of a new Scout Group (including that of a local Venture Scout Unit) without the provisional consent of the District Commissioner, who will decide whether to recommend approval to the District Executive Committee, bearing in mind the number of Groups and the recruitment potential in the locality.

Rule 5 ii   Application for Registration

(a) Application for the registration of a new Scout Group must be made to the District Commissioner by the prospective Scouter.

(b) The District Commissioner and the District Executive Committee must be satisfied that registration is desirable, that the proposed Group or local Unit will be properly conducted, that suitable leaders can be found and that the prospective Scouter in charge of the

Group accepts the Association's policy, undertaking to make his best efforts to:

- form a Group Council and a Group Executive Committee *(See Rules I, 15 and 16)* as soon as possible and in any event within a period of three months from the date of registration;
- give due emphasis to the religious policy of the Association as defined in *Part Two, Rules 1 and 21* of these rules and to the implementation of this policy within the Group;
- initiate a programme of training in accordance with the training policy of the Association as defined in *Part Two* of these rules;
- comply with the provisions of all rules relating to Sponsored Groups, if appropriate.

(c) When he is satisfied that the requirements of *Rule 5 ii (b) above* can be met, the District Commissioner will make a recommendation for registration to his National Headquarters on Form C, sending the form via the County Secretary if the normal practice in the County so requires.

(d) If the District Commissioner refuses to recommend the registration of a Group, he must send a full report on the matter to his Headquarters, through the County Commissioner.

(e) If registration is recommended, the Headquarters of the Association will issue a Notification of Registration and send this, through the District Secretary, to the prospective Scouter in charge of the Group, retaining a copy and sending a further copy to the County Secretary.

Rule 5 iii   Continuance of Registration

(a) It is necessary for the Group to be registered each year by completing Form GR (Annual Registration and Census Return) and paying the annual Membership Subscription in respect of members of the Group *(See also Rule I, 25)*. From the time of the initial registration, it will remain valid until the following 31st March, when it must be renewed.

(b) Groups are only recognised as units of The Scout Association so long as registration is current.

Rule 5 iv   Changes in Registration

(a) If it is required to change the registration of a Group or to amalgamate with another Group, Form C2 must be submitted to his National Headquarters by the District Secretary.

(b) Changes in the composition of a Group made by the addition or loss of Sections within the Group do not necessitate a change of registration. Such changes may be made with the approval of the District Commissioner after consultation with the District Executive Committee and the Sponsoring Authority, if appropriate. No information need be sent to the National Headquarters until the registration is renewed at the end of the normal period through the submission of Form GR *(See Rule 5 iii (a) above)*. If the District Commissioner refuses to approve such a change, he must send a full report to his National Headquarters, through the County Commissioner.

Rule 5 v   Suspension of Registration

(a) A Group may have its registration suspended:

▫ by the District Commissioner or the District Executive Committee who will inform the Sponsoring Authority, if appropriate;

▫ as a result of the suspension of the District *(See Rule I, 33 iv)*. In such a case, the County Commissioner may direct that Groups should not be suspended but attached to a neighbouring District, or to the County as he feels appropriate, for all purposes during the suspension of the District.

(b) In the event of suspension, all Group activities will cease and all Group Scouters are automatically suspended as if each were individually suspended under *Rule 3 x above*. No member of the Group may wear uniform or badges. If the Group Executive Committee is included in the suspension, this must be specified and the District Executive Committee must make arrangements for the administration of Group property and finance during the suspension.

(c) The Group Council will only be included in the suspension if there are special reasons and then only with the approval of the County Commissioner.

(d) Suspension is a purely temporary measure and it must be followed as soon as possible by a full inquiry, convened by the County Secretary as a Committee of Inquiry, which must be conducted in accordance with *Standing Instructions for the Conduct of Committees of Inquiry following Suspension,* copies of which may be obtained from the National Headquarters. The County Commissioner may, however, decide at his discretion that the matter can be resolved without the convening of a Committee of Inquiry if the reason for the suspension is related to a dispute which can be resolved under the provision of *Rule I, 71 ii.*

Rule 5 vi   Cancellation of Registration

The registration of a Scout Group may be cancelled:

□ following the findings of a Committee of Inquiry convened in accordance with *Rule 5 v (d) above;*

- on the recommendation of the District Commissioner and the District Executive Committee, following a meeting of this Committee or of a sub-committee especially convened for this purpose. At such a meeting, the Scouters concerned, the Group Chairman and the Sponsoring Authority, if any, are entitled to be heard;
- if registration is not renewed in accordance with *Rule 5 iii (a) above* at the time of annual registration;
- if the registration of the District is cancelled.

Rule 5 vii   The Suspension and Closure of Sections within a Group

(a) Any Section (i.e. Cub Scout Pack, Scout Troop or Venture Scout Unit) within a Scout Group may be suspended and action must be taken to institute an inquiry as in *Rule 5 v (d) above*.

(b) Such a suspension of a Section may be made by the District Commissioner or the District Executive Committee.

(c) Any Section may be closed by the District Commissioner and the District Executive Committee acting together. Members of the Group for whom membership of a similar Group is not arranged will be deemed to have been dismissed with the rights and consequences provided under *Rule 3 x above* and *Rule I, 9*. Reinstatement, if granted, will be to another Group as directed by the District Commissioner.

(d) Failure to achieve Minimum Standards
A Section may be closed if it is reported for two consecutive years to be below the minimum standard as defined in *Rule I, 7*. It must be closed if it is so reported for three consecutive years. The District Commissioner is responsible for making such reports and closure will be

required by the County Commissioner in accordance with *Rules I, 7 ii (f), I, 7 iii (g)* and *I, 7 iv (e)*.

Rule 6

Group Titles and Specialisations

Rule 6 i

Groups in which the Scout Troop is a Sea or Air Scout Troop may adopt the title Sea Scout Group or Air Scout Group as appropriate.

Rule 6 ii

In such Groups, Cub Scout training remains as in all other Groups and there may be no variation from the approved Cub Scout uniform. Scout training will follow the specialisation of the Group and Venture Scout training may continue the same specialisation, with appropriate variation in the Scout and Venture Scout uniforms.

Rule 7

Composition of the Scout Group

Rule 7 i

(a) A Scout Group consists of one or more of any or all of the following:

Cub Scout Pack

Scout Troop

Venture Scout Unit *(See also Rule I, 7 iv (a))*

(b) A Scout Group is led by a Group Scout Leader with the assistance and support of:

The Group Scouters' Meeting *(See Rule I, 14)*

The Group Council *(See Rule I, 15)*

The Group Executive Committee *(See Rule I, 16)*

Rule 7 ii The Cub Scout Pack

(a) The Cub Scout Pack is made up of a maximum of six *Sixes,* each of which is made up of a *Sixer,* a *Second* and up to four other members.

(b) Sixers are appointed by the Cub Scout Leader. Seconds, who are the Sixers' assistants and deputies, are appointed by the Cub Scout Leader in consultation with the Sixer concerned.

(c) The Sixers' Council

The Sixers' Council consists of the Scouters of the Pack, the Sixers and, if desired, the Seconds.

(d) Cub Scouts wear the approved uniform, with distinguishing emblems and scarves. *(See also Rule 6 ii above.)*

(e) Age Limits for Cub Scouts

The minimum age for entry into the Cub Scout Pack is eight years. The maximum age for membership of the Pack is eleven years and three months. A Cub Scout may transfer to the Scout Troop at any time after reaching the age of ten years and nine months.

The District Commissioner may exercise his discretion in the matter of extending the maximum age limit, guided by the best interests of the boy and the Group if, in his opinion, the circumstances are exceptional.

(f) Minimum Standards for Cub Scout Packs

□ Numbers – An established Cub Scout Pack should have a minimum of twelve Cub Scouts, except in rural and thinly populated and remote areas as defined by the County Commissioner. If the minimum number is lowered by such an exception, arrangements must be made by the leaders in the Group and the District Commissioner for the Pack to meet, at least four times a year, with a Pack from another Group. Where this is not possible, due to the remoteness of the area, special encouragement should be given for the maintenance of the Pack.

□ Leaders – There should be at least two leaders for the Pack, at least one of whom should hold a Warrant.

□ Training – The training of Cub Scouts must be in accordance with *Part Two, Rules 2 – 5* of these rules and there should be at least one whole day Pack expedition each year.

□ Progress – Each year, at least one quarter of the members of the Pack should gain one of the three Cub Scout Progress badges.

The requirements of this rule constitute the minimum standards for Cub Scout Packs. The District Commissioner is required to report annually to the County Commissioner any Cub Scout Pack that does not reach this standard and to assist Packs to reach the required standard where necessary. If the Pack fails to reach the standard for two consecutive years, it may be closed. If it fails to do so for three consecutive years, it will be closed. *(See also Rule 5 vii (d) above.)*

Rule 7 iii   The Scout Troop

(a) The Scout Troop is made up of a number of *Patrols,* each of which is made up of a *Patrol Leader,* an *Assistant Patrol Leader* and up to six other members

(b) Patrol Leaders are appointed by the Scout Leader in consultation with the *Patrol Leaders' Council* and the members of the Patrol. Assistant Patrol Leaders are appointed by the Patrol Leader with the approval of the Scout Leader and the Patrol Leaders' Council, to be the Patrol Leader's assistant and deputy. A *Senior Patrol Leader* may be appointed by the Scout Leader after consultation with the Patrol Leaders' Council.

(c) The Patrol Leaders' Council

The Patrol Leaders' Council is composed of the Patrol Leaders of the Troop, led by the Senior

Patrol Leader if one is appointed. Scouters should attend the Patrol Leaders' Council only in an advisory capacity.

The Patrol Leaders' Council exists to arrange the programme of Troop activities and to attend to Troop administration and expenditure.

(d) The Patrol in Council

The Patrol in Council is a meeting of all the members of the Patrol, called by the Patrol Leader to discuss Patrol affairs.

(e) Scouts wear the approved Scout, Sea Scout or Air Scout uniform with distinguishing emblems and scarves.

(f) Age Limits for Scouts

The minimum age for entry into the Scout Troop is ten years and nine months and the maximum age for membership of the Troop is sixteen years and three months.

While the usual age for transfer to the Venture Scout Unit should be regarded as sixteen years, a Scout may transfer at any time between his fifteenth birthday and the age of sixteen years and three months, provided that the Scout, the Scouters concerned, including the Group Scout Leader where appropriate, and the Unit Executive Committee are all in agreement.

(g) Minimum Standards for Scout Troops

☐ Numbers – An established Scout Troop should have a minimum of twelve Scouts, except in rural and thinly populated and remote areas as defined by the County Commissioner. If the minimum number is lowered by such an exception, arrangements must be made as for Cub Scout Packs *(See Rule 7 ii (f) above)* for meetings with other Scout Troops and for special encouragement for the maintenance of the Troop.

☐ Leaders – There should be at least two leaders for the Troop, at least one of whom should hold a Warrant.

□ Training – The training of Scouts must be in accordance with *Part Two, Rules 6 – 9* of these rules and every member of the Troop must have the opportunity of attending at least one Patrol or Troop camp every year.

□ Progress – Each year, at least one quarter of the Scouts in the Troop should gain one of the three Scout Progress badges.

The requirements of this rule constitute the minimum standards for Scout Troops. The District Commissioner is required to act in regard to Scout Troops in exactly the same way as he acts in regard to Cub Scout Packs under *Rule 7 ii (f) above. See also Rule 5 vii (d) above.*

Rule 7 iv   The Venture Scout Unit

(a) Venture Scout Units may be formed in any one of the following categories:

□ a Unit within a Group;

□ a Unit serving a number of Groups within a locality in the same District;

□ a Unit serving all the Groups in a District;

□ a Unit in a school, Service establishment, industrial or commercial firm, youth centre or similar establishment.

(b) The composition, organisation and administration of a Venture Scout Unit are decided by its Executive Committee, elected by the Venture Scouts of the Unit and consisting of a Unit Chairman and such other members as they may decide.

(c) Venture Scouts wear the approved Venture Scout, Venture Sea Scout or Venture Air Scout uniform as appropriate with distinguishing emblems.

(d) Age Limits for Venture Scouts

The minimum age for entry into the Venture Scout Unit is fifteen years and the maximum age for membership of the Unit is the twentieth birthday. The usual age for entry should be regarded as sixteen years but entry may be permitted at any time after the fifteenth birthday provided that the Scouters concerned, including the Group Scout Leader, and the Unit Executive Committee are all agreed.

(e) Minimum Standards for Venture Scout Units

□ Numbers – An established Venture Scout Unit should have a minimum of nine Venture Scouts, except in rural and thinly populated and remote areas as defined by the County Commissioner. If the minimum number is lowered by such an exception, arrangements must be made as for other Sections *(See Rules 7 ii (f) and 7 iii (g) above)* for meetings with other Venture Scout Units and for special encouragement for the maintenance of the Unit.

□ Leaders – There should be at least two leaders for the Unit, at least one of whom should hold a Warrant.

□ Training – The training of Venture Scouts must be in accordance with *Part Two, Rules 14 – 17* of these rules. The Unit Executive Committee is responsible for organising a worthwhile training programme for a period of up to a year ahead.

The requirements of this rule constitute the minimum standards for Venture Scout Units. The District Commissioner is required to act in regard to Venture Scout Units in exactly the same way as he acts in regard to the other Sections in a Group *(See Rules 7 ii (f) and 7 iii (g) above). (See also Rule 5 vii (d) above).*

(f) Unit Councils

A local Venture Scout Unit (i.e. a Unit which is not a part of a Scout Group composed of various Sections) must have a Group Council *(See Rule I, 15)*. This function may be discharged by the District Scout Council.

*New sub-Rule 7 v. See page 144.

Rule 8   Membership of the Scout Group

Rule 8 i

The admission of any member to the Scout Group rests with the Group Scout Leader, subject, in the case of a Sponsored Group, to the recruitment policy of the Sponsoring Authority. The Group Scout Leader will generally delegate responsibility for admissions to the Scouter in charge of the Section concerned.

Rule 8 ii   Transfers

Cub Scouts, Scouts and Venture Scouts become Members of the Association on joining a Scout Group and forfeit this Membership if they leave the Group. If such a Member leaves due to moving to another locality, the Group Scout Leader should complete a *Transfer Card* and forward it to the District Commissioner of the District into which the Member is moving. If the address of the District Commissioner concerned is not known, the card should be forwarded to the Headquarters of the Association. Transfer Cards should also be sent to the Association's Headquarters in respect of Cub Scouts, Scouts and Venture Scouts who are going to live abroad.

Rule 9   Dismissal of Cub Scouts, Scouts and Venture Scouts

Rule 9 i

No Cub Scout, Scout or Venture Scout may be dismissed from a Scout Group without the approval of the Group Scout Leader. In a Sponsored Group, the Sponsoring Authority must be consulted before such a member is dismissed.

Rule 9 ii   Appeals against Dismissal

Any Cub Scout, Scout or Venture Scout who is dismissed has the right of appeal to the District Commissioner, who may, if so requested by the person dismissed, appoint a committee to hear the appeal. Reasonable opportunity must be given for the dismissed person to attend the meeting of such a committee to state his case. If the dismissal is from a Sponsored Group, the Sponsoring Authority, who will have already been consulted in accordance with *Rule 4 ii (c) above,* has the right to attend and be heard by the committee. The Headquarters of the Association will issue instructions to District Commissioners on request.

Rule 10 · The Appointment of Leaders in the Scout Group

Rule 10 i

The appointment of Group Scout Leaders, Leaders of Sections and Assistant Leaders is made by the following procedure:

(a) Enquiry

No prospective leader may commence working in a Scout Group until the following enquiry procedure has been completed, unless the person has been introduced to the District by the Association's Headquarters in a written statement as to the person's suitability.

When any person whose character and antecedents are not known or any person who has returned to a locality after a period of residence elsewhere offers or seeks to serve the Association by joining a Scout Group as a leader or Instructor or to act in any administrative capacity within the Group, the offer or request must be reported at once to the District Commissioner. The District Commissioner must at once consult the Association's Headquarters, using Form WE. In the absence of the District Commissioner or any Assistant District Commissioner, or if circumstances are urgent, the Group Scout Leader must write at once to the Association's Headquarters, using the First Class letter service and marking the envelope *Private and Confidential.*

Whether this enquiry is initiated on Form WE by the District Commissioner or by letter by the Group Scout Leader, the fullest possible information about the person must be given.

(b) At the same time as this enquiry is initiated, local references must be sought to ascertain the person's suitability. In the event of such local references establishing that the person is not suitable, full details must be sent by the District Secretary to the Association's Headquarters in a letter marked *Private and Confidential* and the District Commissioner must be informed.

Local references need not be sought if the person is known to be of such good standing in the locality that this would not be necessary.

Rule 10 ii Application for Appointment

(a) Application for appointment as a leader is made on Form LS which is submitted to the Association's Headquarters after completion and signing by the applicant. The applicant should be introduced to the people with whom he or she will be most closely concerned in the proposed initial appointment. In the case of prospective Group Scout Leaders, the applicant must be introduced to the District Commissioner, the Assistant District Commissioner (Leader Training) and the Sponsoring Authority, if appropriate. In the case of prospective Section Leaders and Assistant Leaders, the applicant must be introduced to the Group Scout Leader and the Sponsoring Authority, if appropriate, as well as to the Assistant District Commissioner with responsibility for the Section concerned and the Assistant District Commissioner (Leader Training).

(b) The completed Form LS must be sent to the District Secretary or the Secretary of the District Appointments Sub-Committee as soon as possible. If the applicant's character and antecedents are not known, the Secretary will arrange for references to be provided and will make available to the members of the Sub-Committee the report received from the Association's Headquarters in reply to the enquiry made on Form WE.

(c) Responsibilities of District Commissioners in Appointments

The District Commissioner and the District Appointments Sub-Committee must each be satisfied that:

☐ the applicant is within the prescribed age limits for the appointment *(See Rule I, 13)*;

☐ the applicant is suitable in character and antecedents to be entrusted with the care of boys;

☐ the applicant has the necessary qualifications to carry out the duties of the appointment *(See Rule I, 13)*;

☐ the applicant understands and accepts the aims of the Association;

☐ the applicant understands the Leader Training obligations which apply to the appointment.

(d) If the Appointments Sub-Committee supports the applications, the following procedure is followed:

☐ the Secretary signs Form LS;

☐ the District Commissioner signs the Form LS if he approves the application;

☐ the form is sent to the Association's Headquarters, who will issue a Warrant;

☐ on receipt of the Warrant, the District Secretary writes in the initial appointment, records the appointment in the District records and passes the Warrant to the District Commissioner for presentation to the new leader.

(e) If the Appointments Sub-Committee does not support the application, the Secretary will inform the District Commissioner who, if he agrees with the Sub-Committee's conclusion, must submit, with the Secretary, a full report to the Association's Headquarters, marked *Private and Confidential*.

(f) If the District Commissioner does not agree with the conclusion of the Sub-Committee, the application must be considered by the District Executive Committee. In the event of the District Commissioner not agreeing with that Committee's decision, the matter should be referred to the County Commissioner, whose decision must be accepted as final by all parties.

Rule 10 iii   Presentation of Warrants

Warrants must be presented by the District Commissioner, or, exceptionally, by an Assistant District Commissioner, as soon as possible after receipt. The leader is invested and makes or reaffirms the Scout Promise when he receives his Warrant.

Rule 10 iv   Continuance of Appointments

(a) Warrants remain valid until 31st March in the fifth year following the year of issue, when they must be reviewed by the District Commissioner and the District Appointments Sub-Committee.

*Sub-Rule 10 iv (b) amended. See page 135.

(b) The renewal of Warrants is subject to the satisfactory completion of Leader Training appropriate to the appointment as follows:

□ Group Scout Leaders and Section Leaders must complete the appropriate Basic Training within three years of appointment and the appropriate Advanced Training within five years of appointment or of completing Basic Training, whichever is the later.

□ A Scouter who is not a Section Leader must complete the appropriate Basic Training within three years of appointment.

(c) Renewal of Warrants

Subject to the Scouter having met the training obligations of his appointment, his Warrant may be renewed at the time of its expiry by the District Commissioner and the District Appointments Sub-Committee. The District Commissioner should be satisfied that the

Scouter still meets the requirements of *Rule 10 ii (c) above.*

Rule 10 v   Changes in Appointments within the Scout District

(a) Appointments may be changed by the District Commissioner and the District Appointments Sub-Committee subject to the approval of the Group Scout Leader and the Sponsoring Authority, if appropriate.

(b) The new appointment must be entered on the Warrant by the District Secretary, who must also amend the District Records.

Rule 10 vi Ceasing to hold an Appointment

(a) On ceasing to hold an appointment, a Scouter must surrender his Warrant to the District Secretary, who will complete Form W and send it to the Association's Headquarters.

(b) If the Scouter's service has been satisfactory, the District Secretary will cancel the Warrant and return it to the Scouter. Otherwise, the cancelled Warrant will be sent to the Association's Headquarters with the Form W via the County Commissioner.

Rule 10 vii   Cancellation of Warrants

A Warrant may be cancelled, on the recommendation of the District Commissioner, by the Association's Headquarters on the following grounds:

- that the holder wishes to resign;
- that the holder acquiesces when notified that a recommendation is to be made for the cancellation of his Warrant;
- that the holder is not within the age limits prescribed for the appointment *(See Rule I, 13);*

- that the Warrant is not to be renewed when reviewed under *Rule 10 iv (c) above*;
- that the holder has discontinued or failed to perform his duties;
- that the Association's Headquarters confirms the cancellation of the Warrant following suspension *(See Rules 3 x and 5 v above)*.

Rule 10 viii Limitation of Appointments

No Scouter may hold more than one appointment unless he is able to carry out all the duties of more than one appointment satisfactorily. The District Commissioner must give approval for any person to hold more than one appointment and, if the appointments are to be held in more than one District or County, the approval of all the Commissioners concerned must be obtained.

Rule 11

The Appointment of Instructors

★Sub-Rule 11 i amended. See page 144.

Rule 11 i

Instructors, other than Cub Scout and Occasional Instructors, are appointed and retired by the Group Scout Leader subject to the approval of the District Commissioner and the District Appointments Sub-Committee. The appointment must be reviewed every five years and may be renewed.

★Sub-Rule 11 ii amended. See page 144.

Rule 11 ii Cub Scout Instructors

(a) Cub Scout Instructors are appointed and retired by the Cub Scout Leader with the approval of:
- the Venture Scout Leader, in the case of Venture Scouts who are Cub Scout Instructors;

□ the Guider and Scout District Commissioner concerned, in the case of Ranger Guides who are Cub Scout Instructors;

□ the District Commissioner and the Group Scout Leader, in the case of others.

(b) Cub Scout Instructors should attend a Cub Scout Instructors' Course as soon as possible after appointment.

Rule 11 iii   Occasional Instructors

Occasional Instructors are specialist instructors (e.g. in rock climbing, canoeing) who are appointed and retired by the District Commissioner.

Rule 11 iv   Ceasing to Hold an Instructor Appointment

Instructor appointments may be terminated on the following grounds:

□ that the Instructor wishes to resign;

□ that the Instructor acquiesces when notified that a recommendation is to be made for the termination of the appointment;

□ that the period of the appointment has expired and it is not to be renewed;

□ that the holder has discontinued or failed to perform the duties of the appointment;

□ that the Association's Headquarters confirms the termination of the appointment following suspension *(See Rules 3 x and 5 v above)*.

Rule 12   Physically Handicapped Adults

Rule 12 i

Persons subject to a physical handicap may

apply to the appropriate authority for appointment as Instructors (including Cub Scout and Occasional Instructors), Administrators, Assistant Leaders and, exceptionally, as Leaders. Full details of the nature and effects of the handicap must be given.

Rule 12 ii

The District Commissioner must satisfy himself that a physically handicapped person appointed as in *Rule 12 i above,* is physically capable of maintaining the supervision and attention required.

Rule 13 Qualifications and Responsibilities of Appointments

Rule 13 i   The Group Scout Leader

(a) Age Limits

The minimum age for appointment as a Group Scout Leader is thirty; if specially recommended by the District Commissioner to the Appointments Sub-Committee, a younger man may be appointed, but no one younger than twenty-five years of age may be appointed. The maximum age limit is sixty-five.

(b) Responsibilities

The Group Scout Leader is responsible for:
- the continuity and development of training in the Sections of the Group;
- maintaining effective communication with the District Commissioner, the youth service, the District Scout Fellowship *(See Rule I, 51)* and other organisations whose advice and support can be of use to the Group;
- acting as Chairman of the Group Scouters'

Meeting *(See Rule I, 14)* and encouraging co-operation among the Scouters of the Group;

□ nominating the Group Chairman *(See Rule I, 18)*. The Group Scout Leader may not hold this appointment himself, nor may he nominate a Scouter;

□ matters relating to the admission and Membership of Cub Scouts, Scouts and Venture Scouts in the Group;

□ all other matters specified in these rules for Group Scout Leaders.

(c) The Assistant Group Scout Leader

An Assistant Group Scout Leader may be appointed, with responsibilities as defined by the Group Scout Leader, who should have regard to the desirability of developing the Assistant's leadership potential. The age limits for such an appointment are the same as for the appointment of Group Scout Leaders *(See Rule 13 i (a) above)*.

(d) Scouter in Charge

If there is no Group Scout Leader, the District Commissioner may appoint one of the Scouters of the Group to act as Scouter in Charge. Such an appointment may carry any or all of the responsibilities defined in *Rule 13 i (b) above,* as specified by the District Commissioner.

*New sub-Rule 13 ii. See page 145. Present sub-Rule 13 ii now renumbered as 13 iv.

Rule 13 ii   The Cub Scout Leader

(a) Age Limits

The age limits for the appointment of Cub Scout Leaders are:

Minimum: twenty

Maximum: sixty-five

(b) Responsibilities

The Cub Scout Leader is responsible for the training of Cub Scouts, subject to the general supervision of the Group Scout Leader and with the assistance of Assistant Cub Scout

44

Leaders, Instructors and Cub Scout Instructors.

*New sub-Rule 13 iii. See page 145. Present sub-Rule 13 iii now renumbered as 13 v.

Rule 13 iii Assistant Cub Scout Leaders

(a) Age Limits

The age limits for the appointment of Assistant Cub Scout Leaders are:

Minimum: eighteen

Maximum: sixty-five

(b) Responsibilities

The responsibilities of Assistant Cub Scout Leaders are specified by the Cub Scout Leader, who should have regard to the desirability of developing the Assistant's leadership potential.

*Present sub-Rule 13 iv now renumbered as 13 vi.

Rule 13 iv Cub Scout Instructors

(a) Age Limits

The appointment of Cub Scout Instructor may be held by:

- □ Venture Scouts;
- □ Ranger Guides over sixteen years of age;
- □ other young persons over sixteen years of age.

The maximum age for a Cub Scout Instructor is twenty years. Instructors who have been working with a Pack up to their twentieth birthday may continue to do so but will hold the title of *Instructor* and not Cub Scout Instructor.

(b) Responsibilities

The responsibilities of Cub Scout Instructors are specified by the Cub Scout Leader at the time of appointment. Cub Scout Instructors may not carry any responsibility for the management of the Pack.

*Present sub-Rule 13 v now renumbered as 13 vii.

Rule 13 v The Scout Leader

(a) Age Limits

The age limits for the appointment of Scout Leaders are:

Minimum: twenty
Maximum: sixty-five
(b) Responsibilities
The Scout Leader is responsible for the training of Scouts, subject to the general supervision of the Group Scout Leader and with the assistance of Assistant Scout Leaders and Instructors.

*Sub-Rule
13 v (b)
amended.
See page 143.

Rule 13 vi   Assistant Scout Leaders

*Present sub-
Rule 13 vi
now
renumbered
as 13 viii.

(a) Age Limits
The age limits for the appointment of Assistant Scout Leaders are:
Minimum: eighteen
Maximum: sixty-five
(b) Responsibilities
The responsibilities of Assistant Scout Leaders are specified by the Scout Leader, who should have regard to the desirability of developing the Assistant's leadership potential.

Rule 13 vii   The Venture Scout Leader

*Present sub-
Rule 13 vii
now
renumbered
as 13 ix.

(a) Age Limits
The age limits for the appointment of Venture Scout Leaders are:
Minimum: twenty-one
Maximum: sixty-five
(b) Responsibilities
The Venture Scout Leader is responsible for the training of Venture Scouts, subject to the general supervision of the Group Scout Leader if the Unit is part of a larger Group or of the District Commissioner if it is a local Venture Scout Unit. He will be assisted by Assistant Venture Scout Leaders and Instructors.

*Sub-Rule
13 vii (b)
amended.
See page 143.

Rule 13 viii   Assistant Venture Scout Leaders

*Present sub-
Rule 13 viii
now
renumbered
as 13 x.

(a) Age Limits
The age limits for the appointment of Assistant

Venture Scout Leaders are:

Minimum: twenty

Maximum: sixty-five

(b) Responsibilities

The responsibilities of Assistant Venture Scout Leaders are specified by the Venture Scout Leader, who should have regard to the desirability of developing the Assistant's leadership potential.

*Present sub-Rule 13 ix now renumbered as 13 xi.

Rule 13 ix Qualifications and Responsibilities of Instructor Appointments

(a) Age Limits

The age limits for the appointment of Instructors and Occasional Instructors are:

Minimum: seventeen

Maximum: sixty-five

(b) Responsibilities

Instructors and Occasional Instructors are responsible for aspects of training and specialist badge instruction as specified at the time of their appointment. They may not carry any responsibility for the management within the Group.

Rule 14 · The Group Scouters' Meeting

Rule 14 i

The Group Scouters' Meeting is held as frequently as necessary and is led by the Group Scout Leader. Its purpose is to:

- concern itself with the well-being and development of each member of the Group;
- ensure the progress and continuity of all training in the Group;
- plan and co-ordinate all the Group's activities;
- keep the Group Executive Committee advised of the financial requirements of the training programme

Rule 14 ii   Membership of the Group Scouters' Meeting

All Warrant holders and the Chairman of the Executive Committee of any Venture Scout Unit in the Group may attend the Group Scouters' Meeting.

Rule 15 · The Group Council

Rule 15 i

The Group Council is the electoral body which supports Scouting in the locality through the Scout Group. Under the chairmanship of the Group Chairman, it must hold an Annual General Meeting in May or as soon as possible thereafter each year to:

- approve the Annual Report of the Group Executive Committee, including the audited accounts;
- approve the Group Scout Leader's nomination of the Group Chairman and nominated

members of the Group Executive Committee;

□ elect a Group Secretary and a Group Treasurer *(See Rules I, 19 ii and iii)*;

□ elect certain members of the Group Executive Committee. *(See Rule I, 16 ii)*.

Rule 15 ii   Membership of the Group Council

Membership of the Group Council is open to:

□ Scouters, Instructors (including Cub Scout Instructors), Administrators and Advisers;

□ Venture Scouts;

□ Patrol Leaders;

□ parents of Cub Scouts, Scouts and Venture Scouts who are members of the Group;

□ the Sponsoring Authority or his nominee;

□ former Scouts and their parents and other supporters of the Group appointed by the Group Scout Leader, the Group Executive Committee or the Group Council.

Members of the Group Council who are not Members of the Association may wear the Associate's lapel badge. They do not pay the annual Membership Subscription.

Rule 15 iii   Ceasing to be a member of the Group Council

Membership of the Group Council ceases upon:

□ the resignation of the member;

□ the dissolution of the Council;

□ the termination of such membership by the Association's Headquarters following a recommendation by the Group Executive Committee.

Rule 16

The Group Executive Committee

Rule 16 i

The Group Executive Committee is the business management committee of the Group. It is responsible for:

- the maintenance of Group property;
- assisting the Group Scout Leader in finance, public relations, accommodation, camping grounds and adult support, including the recruitment of leaders;
- appointing any sub-committees that may be required;
- appointing Group Administrators and Advisers other than those who are elected *(See Rule I, 18 ii)*.

Rule 16 ii   Membership of the Group Executive Committee

Ex officio members
The Group Chairman
The Group Scout Leader
The Assistant Group Scout Leader (if any)
All Section Leaders
The Group Secretary
The Group Treasurer
A nominee of the Sponsoring Authority (if any).
(See also Rule I, 36 i (e), I, 40 i (b), I, 58 i (b) and I, 63 ii (c)).
Nominated members
Members of the Group Council nominated by the Group Scout Leader and approved by the Group Council, including a parent of at least one Cub Scout, one Scout and one Venture Scout (if there is a Venture Scout Unit in the Group) from the Group.

Elected members
Members of the Group Council elected annually by the Council. The number of elected members may not exceed the number of members nominated by the Group Scout Leader.

Co-opted members
Members co-opted annually by the Committee. The number of co-opted members may not exceed the number of members nominated by the Group Scout Leader.

Rule 16 iii   Membership of Sub-Committees of the Group Executive Committee

(a) The Group Scout Leader, the Assistant Group Scout Leader (if any) and the Group Chairman are ex officio members of any sub-committee of the Group Executive Committee.

(b) Any Fund Raising Sub-Committee must include at least two members of the Group Executive Committee, in addition to the Group Scout Leader and the Assistant Group Scout Leader (if any), who are ex officio members of such a sub-committee. No other Scouters may serve on such a sub-committee.

Rule 17   Conduct of Meetings in the Scout Group

Rule 17 i
In meetings of the Group Council and the Group Executive Committee, only ex officio members, elected members, nominated members and co-opted members may vote.

Rule 17 ii
Decisions are made by a majority of votes. In

the event of an equal number of votes being cast on either side in any issue, the Chairman does not have a casting vote but the matter is taken not to have been carried.

Rule 17 iii

The Group Council must make a resolution defining the quorum for meetings of the Group Council and the Group Executive Committee and its sub-committees.

Rule 18 Administrators and Advisers in the Scout Group – Appointment

Rule 18 i

The Group Chairman, the Group Secretary and the Group Treasurer are appointed by the following procedures:

(a) The Group Chairman

The Group Chairman is nominated by the Group Scout Leader and his appointment is approved by the Group Council at its Annual General Meeting.

(b) The Group Secretary and the Group Treasurer

The Group Secretary and the Group Treasurer are elected by the Group Council at its Annual General Meeting.

Rule 18 ii   Other Administrators and Advisers

Other Administrators and Advisers may be appointed by the Group Executive Committee if it so wishes, subject to the approval of the Group Scout Leader. Such appointments are governed by conditions made at the time of appointment.

Rule 18 iii   Enquiry

The enquiry procedure detailed in *Rule 10 i above* must be followed in appointing all Group Administrators and Advisers.

Rule 18 iv   Age Limits

The minimum age for appointment as a Group Administrator or Adviser is seventeen years. There is no maximum age limit.

Rule 18 v   Recording of Administrator and Adviser Appointments

The District Secretary must keep a record of all Group Administrator and Adviser appointments.

Rule 18 vi   Termination of Administrator and Adviser Appointments

The appointments of Administrators and Advisers may be terminated by:

- the resignation of the holder;
- the holder acquiescing when notified that a recommendation is to be made for the termination of his appointment by the Group Executive Committee;
- the expiry of the period of the appointment;
- confirmation by the Association's Headquarters of the termination of the appointment following suspension *(See Rules 3 x and 5 v above)*.

Rule 19   Responsibilities of Group Administrators

Rule 19 i   The Group Chairman

The Group Chairman is appointed to work closely with the Group Scout Leader in the administration of the Group with the object of creating the best possible circumstances and facilities for the training programme in the Group. He acts as Chairman of the Group Council and of the Group Executive Committee.

Rule 19 ii   The Group Secretary

(a) The Group Secretary is appointed to:

□ act as Secretary to the Group Council and the Group Executive Committee;

□ keep such records concerning the administration and training in the Group as the Group Scout Leader or the Group Chairman may require;

□ make available to members of the Group information and instructions from Headquarters, the County and the District or from any other body;

□ perform all other duties specified in these rules for Group Secretaries.

(b) The office of Group Secretary may not be held by a Scouter and may not be combined with that of Group Treasurer.

Rule 19 iii   The Group Treasurer

(a) The Group Treasurer is appointed to:

□ advise the Group Executive Committee on

financial control and expenditure and to produce an annual budget after consultation with the Group Executive Committee and the Group Scouters' Meeting

□ receive all monies from Sections in the Group on behalf of the Group Executive Committee and to keep account of all funds;

□ pay out money as authorised by the Group Executive Committee;

□ open such bank accounts as may be necessary in the name of the Group *(See Rule I, 22)*;

□ ensure that funds allotted to Sections in the Group are properly accounted for;

□ invest, in consultation with the Group Executive Committee, any accumulated funds in accordance with *Rule I, 28 xi;*

□ work closely with the Group Council and the District Treasurer in all matters related to the raising of funds;

□ supervise the administration of Group property and equipment and ensure that proper inventories are maintained and proper insurance arranged;

□ perform all other duties specified in these rules for Group Treasurers.

(b) The office of Group Treasurer may not be held by a Scouter and may not be combined with that of Group Secretary.

Rule 20

Finance – General

Rule 20 i

Every Scout Group or local Venture Scout Unit is a separate educational charity and is under a statutory obligation to keep proper books of account, to send statements of account on request to the Charity Commissioners and to have its accounts audited. These are requirements under the Charities Act, 1960 and under this rule.

Rule 20 ii

Group Treasurers and other administrators concerned with finance must ensure that proper budgeting and control operate in the Group *(See Rule 19 iii above)* and must consult the Group Executive Committee and the Group Scouters' Meeting on the financial aspects of planning the Group's activities.

Rule 20 iii

Group Treasurers and other administrators concerned with finance must keep account books and records to enable them to send a statement of accounts annually to the District Treasurer or when called upon to do so by the Association's Headquarters or by the Charity Commissioners. The following information must be readily available:

- particulars of assets and, in the case of assets other than equipment, particulars of the trustees in whom they are vested *(See Rule I, 28)* as at 31st March or other date concluding the preceding accounting year;

- assets forming part of a permanent endowment (i.e. property held by the Group which may not be sold or disposed of) should be shown separately;

- a statement of liabilities on the same date;

- a statement of receipts during the year ending on the same date, classified as to the nature of the receipt, showing separately receipts which form part of a permanent endowment, if any;

- a statement of payments made during the year ending on the same date, classified as to the nature of the payment, showing separately payments made out of a permanent endowment, if any.

Rule 20 iv

A statement as described in *Rule 20 iii above,* duly audited, must be submitted by each Group to the District Treasurer by not later than 31st July each year. The auditor must be an independent and responsible person but need not be a qualified accountant.

Rule 21 Maintaining Group Accounts

Rule 21 i

Each Section of a Scout Group must itself administer any subscriptions paid by its members as well as sums allotted for current expenses by the Group Executive Committee. If substantial sums are handled by the Section, a bank account should be opened in accordance with *Rule I, 22*.

Rule 21 ii

Where no Section bank account exists, special subscriptions paid by members of the Section or their parents (e.g. instalments towards the cost of an expedition or payments of the annual Membership Subscription) must be handed to the Group Treasurer as soon as possible after receipt. The Group Treasurer must keep such records of account as are necessary for this purpose and, having recorded the receipt, must pay the money into the Group bank account.

Rule 21 iii

Each Section must keep a proper cash account which must be produced, together with any cash balance and supporting vouchers at the request of the Group Treasurer as often as the Group Executive Committee may decide but, in any event, not less frequently than once every three months.

Rule 21 iv

Funds administered by Sections must be shown in the Group Treasurer's accounts and must be included in the Group's annual statement and balance sheet.

Rule 22

Bank Accounts

Rule 22 i

All money received by or on behalf of a Scout Group, Group Council or Group Executive Committee must be paid into a bank account held in the name of the Group, except as provided in *Rule 21 above*. This account may be a National Savings Bank Account or a Trustee Savings Bank Account. The account must be operated by not less than two signatories, authorised by the Group Executive Committee.

Rule 22 ii

No money received by any Section or by the Group Council or the Group Executive Committee may be paid into any person's private bank account.

*Addition to sub-Rule 22 iii. See page 136.

Rule 22 iii

Funds being accumulated for a special purpose (e.g. a building fund) and other available funds must be paid into a bank deposit account held in the name of the Group and operated by not less than two signatories, authorised by the Group Executive Committee. If such funds are to be held for a prolonged period, they must be properly invested in the names of trustees *(See Rule I, 29)* or of The Scout Association Trust Corporation *(See Rule I, 28 ii (b)* and *Rule I, 86 ii)*.

Rule 22 iv

The bank at which the Group account is held must be instructed to send to the Group Chairman a copy of the statement of the account as at 31st March or other date concluding the financial year. If more than one account is held by the Group or Sections of the Group, copies of all the statements of account must be sent as at the same date.

Rule 23

Group Accounts – Disposal of Assets

Rule 23 i   Disposal of Assets at Amalgamation

(a) If two or more Scout Groups amalgamate, the retiring Treasurers must prepare a statement of account as detailed in *Rule 20 iii above*, dated at the date of the amalgamation. This statement must be handed, together with all Group assets, supported by all books of account and vouchers, to the Treasurer of the new Group.

(b) If the Treasurer of the new Group considers it necessary after consultation with the Group Executive Committee, he may ask the District Executive Committee to appoint an auditor to examine the accounts.

Rule 23 ii   Disposal of Assets at Closure

If a Group ceases to exist, the Group Treasurer must prepare a statement of account as detailed in *Rule 20 iii above*, dated at the effective date of closure. This statement, together with all Group assets, must be handed to the District Treasurer as soon as possible after the closure date and must be supported by all books of account and vouchers. The District Treasurer will check the statement, or will have it checked, and if, in consultation with the District Executive Committee, he decides that a formal audit is desirable, he will arrange for this to be carried out. When he is satisfied that the statement shows the true state of the Group's financial position at the date of closure, he must forward a copy of the statement to his National Headquarters, requesting instructions for the disposal of the Group's assets and books of account.

Rule 24   Preservation of Books of Account

Books and statements of account must be preserved for not less than seven years from the date of the first entry.

Rule 25   Payment of the Membership Subscription

*Sub-Rule 25 i amended. See page 145.

Rule 25 i

In order to meet the costs of Headquarters services and the costs of organising and administering the Association nationally and to provide for meeting the Association's obligations to World Scouting, every Scout Group and local Venture Scout Unit is required to pay each year the Membership Subscription, the amount of which is decided by the Committee of the Council of the Association, in respect of members of the Group or Unit who are shown on the Annual Registration and Census Return in the following categories:

- □ Cub Scouts
- □ Scouts
- □ Venture Scouts
- □ Scouters

□ Instructors and Cub Scout Instructors (excluding Occasional Instructors)

Rule 25 ii

The sum decided by the Committee of the Council applies to the whole of the United Kingdom but the Committee will decide what proportion, if any, is to be retained by the National Councils of Scotland and Northern Ireland towards the costs of their own Headquarters services.

Rule 25 iii   Membership Subscription – Extension Groups

Registered Extension Groups must pay the annual Membership Subscription in respect of their members in the categories specified in *Rule 25 i above,* but, under special circumstances, such Groups may apply through the District Commissioner, for partial or total exemption from this payment.

*New sub-Rule 25 iv. See page 146.

(*See also Rule, I, 45* and *I, 65*)

Rule 26

Fund Raising in the Scout Group

Rule 26 i

In order to maintain its work and to provide all that is needed to implement its training programme, The Scout Association has to support itself financially. Within this commitment, Scout Groups are expected to provide sufficient funds to carry out their own programme of activities and to participate in financing the Association as a whole.

Rule 26 ii

Fund raising carried out on behalf of Scouting

must be conducted in accordance with the principles embodied in the Scout Promise and Law.

Rule 26 iii

The raising of funds is largely a matter for the attention of adults working in support of Scouting through the Group Council, but Cub Scouts, Scouts and Venture Scouts may participate in fund raising provided that such activities do not take precedence over their training. Where they do engage in fund raising, as in Scout Job Week (details of which are announced annually by the Association's Headquarters) they must earn money rather than solicit gratuitous payments.

Rule 26 iv

When entering into any obligation or commitment connected with fund raising with another party (e.g. when ordering fund raising materials) the person concerned must make it clear to the other party that he is acting on behalf of the Group and not in his personal capacity.

Rule 26 v

All fund raising undertaken on behalf of the Association must be carried out in accordance with the spirit of Statutes and enactments governing particular activities. Attention is particularly drawn to:

□ The House to House Collections Act, 1939;
□ The Children and Young Persons Act, 1963, as amended;
□ The Lotteries and Amusement Act 1976 and Gaming Act 1968.

Rule 26 vi   Betting, Gaming and Lotteries

(a) If a Group considers raising funds by means governed by the provisions of the Lotteries and Amusement Act 1976 and Gaming Act 1968, the proposed activity must have the approval of the Group Executive Committee and the Sponsoring Authority, if any, and of the District Commissioner and District Chairman. Regard must be paid to the views of parents and to local public opinion. Activities affected by this legislation include raffles, whist drives and similar methods of fund raising involving participation on payment of stakes.

(b) The Group Executive Committee will be the promoter of any fund raising activity governed by the Acts.

(c) Scout units in the areas adjacent to that of the Group engaging in fund raising should be informed of the proposed activity and care must be taken to contain the activity within as close an area to that in which the Group operates as is practicable.

(d) Any advertising material used must conform with the requirements of the Acts and must not contain any matter which is not in strict conformity with the standards of the Association.

Rule 26 vii Methods of Fund Raising

(a) The provisions of this rule govern the selection of methods of fund raising and are designed to allow as much local initiative as possible, consistent with the interests of the Association's reputation and good standing.

(b) Fund raising conducted on behalf of Scouting may be by any means not forbidden by law, provided that:

▢ the proceeds of the activity go wholly to

support the work of the Group or, in the case of approved joint activities with other organisations, that part of the proceeds allotted to the Group is applied wholly to the work of the Group *(See Rule I, 26 viii)*;

□ it is not conducive to encouraging the habit of gambling.

Rule 26 viii   Joint Fund Raising Projects

Joint fund raising projects with other charitable organisations are permitted provided that the part of the proceeds allotted to the other organisation is used wholly for purposes other than those of private gain. The National Headquarters should be consulted if there is the slightest doubt as to the bona fides of the other organisation in respect of the purposes of the fund raising activity.

Rule 26 ix   Appeals for Funds

(a) Groups may not issue general appeals for funds, except in exceptional circumstances with the approval of the District Commissioner and the District Executive Committee, who must invariably consult the County Commissioner and National Headquarters.

(b) Any such appeal which may be permitted must be made only in a specified area which must not exceed the boundaries of the District in which the Group is located.

Rule 27   Grant Aid and Loans

Rule 27 i

Provided that a Group raises a proportion of its own funds, it may accept financial assistance in the form of Grant Aid or loans.

Rule 27 ii
Applications for grants from education authorities must be supported by the District Commissioner and the County Commissioner before submission to Local Education Authorities.

Rule 27 iii
Applications for grants from the Association's Headquarters must have the approval of the District Commissioner and the County Commissioner.

Rule 27 iv
Applications for grants from sources other than those referred to in *Rules 27 ii* and *27 iii above*, must have the approval of the District Commissioner and of the County Commissioner if the latter so directs.
(See also Rule I, 47 and I, 67.)

Rule 28 Trusteeship, Property and Equipment

Rule 28 i
This rule does not apply in Scotland.
Scout Groups must be properly accommodated and equipped in order to carry out their training programmes and the administrators of the Group must concern themselves with all legal requirements relevant to the ownership of all property and equipment or to the hiring of premises.

*Sub-Rule 28 ii (a) amended. See page 136.

Rule 28 ii
(a) All property, including freehold or leasehold premises, land, buildings used under

formal licence, investments and accumulated funds and substantial quantities of equipment must be held on behalf of the Association by trustees appointed as specified in *Rule I, 28 ii (b)*.

(b) Trustees must be appointed under a Declaration of Trust. They may be two or more people nominated by the Group Executive Committee or a Trust Corporation licensed by the Lord Chancellor. The Scout Association Trust Corporation, which is so licensed, may be appointed for this purpose.

*Sub-Rule 28 ii (c) amended. See page 136.

(c) Trusteeship must be in accordance with the Association's model Declaration of Trust, details of which can be obtained from the Association's Headquarters. If a Trust Corporation is appointed, it will hold the property upon trusts laid down in the appropriate Scout Trust Deed, details of which can be obtained from the Association's Headquarters.

*Sub-Rule 28 ii (d) amended. See page 136.

(d) If circumstances appear to make it necessary or desirable that property be held upon trusts other than those laid down in the appropriate Scout Trust Deed, or that it be held upon special trusts, the matter should be referred to the Association's Headquarters.

Rule 28 iii   The Charities Act, 1960

This rule applies in England and Wales only

(a) The Secretary of a Group which owns or occupies land and/or buidings, or which has a permanent endowment, must apply for registration as an educational charity to the Charity Commissioners. In the case of a Group which has vested trusteeship in The Scout Association Trust Corporation, this application will be made on behalf of the Group by the Corporation.

(b) The Group Secretary must ensure that all statutory duties and obligations imposed by the Charities Act, 1960, are fulfilled.

Rule 28 iv

Land or buildings vested in trustees should be in freehold possession or leased for a certain number of years and must have been properly conveyed, leased or assigned.

Rule 28 v

The Group Treasurer must ensure that an acceptable valuation is attributed to property owned or leased by the Group by the Valuation Department of the Inland Revenue in order to obtain proper relief or exemption from the General Rate.

Rule 28 vi

Land and/or buildings must not be occupied by the Group without formal written licence if the occupation is to be for a substantial period or if any payment is to be made in respect of the occupation.

Rule 28 vii

If land and/or buildings are held on a lease of less than seven years, special consideration must be given by the Group Executive Committee to proposals for capital expenditure on buildings or other improvements.

Rule 28 viii   Property – Sponsored Groups

Agreements with Sponsoring Authorities *(See Rule 4 v above)* identify and distinguish property belonging to the Sponsoring Organisation and that belonging to the Association. Property owned by the Group as recorded in such agreements must be administered as required by these rules.

Rule 28 ix   Disposal of Property

(a) Disposal of Property at Amalgamation

The model Declaration of Trust and the Scout

Trust Deeds referred to in *Rule 28 ii (c) above*, contain certain provisions for the amalgamation of Groups. The retiring Secretaries of Groups which are amalgamating must hand to the Secretary of the new Group all documents of title and the keys to any buildings to which the former Groups had right *(See also Rule 23 i above)*. Any difficulties encountered in the transfer of property at amalgamation should be referred to the National Headquarters.

(b) Disposal of Property at Closure

The property of a Group which closes or is closed must be disposed of as instructed by Headquarters after receipt of the final statement of accounts required under *Rule 23 ii above*. Until these instructions are received, the District Executive Committee must take all necessary steps to ensure the preservation of the property and documents of title.

*Sub-Rule 28 x amended. See page 137.

Rule 28 x   Joint Occupation of Premises by Scout and Girl Guide Units

A special Declaration of Trust, which must provide for the formation of a joint management committee, must be drawn up if premises are to be occupied jointly by Scout and Girl Guide units. This does not apply if the premises are used jointly under licence or if the premises are occupied by other similar arrangements. A copy of the appropriate Declaration of Trust can be obtained from the Association's Headquarters

Rule 28 xi   Investments

(a) Powers of investment are conferred upon The Scout Association by its Royal Charter and these powers may be delegated to specific Scout Groups by the Committee of the Council of the Association. Such delegation of investment powers will be recorded in a special constitution and the Treasurer of such a Group must ensure that any powers so delegated are not exceeded.

(b) In Groups other than those on which the Committee of the Council has specifically conferred investment powers, the Group Treasurer must ensure that investments acquired comply with the Trustee Investments Act, 1961 and/or any other Act of Parliament in force relating to the investment of trustee or charitable funds. He must obtain refunds from the Inland Revenue of tax deducted at source on investment income.

(c) Investments held on behalf of Groups must be registered in such a way as to show that they are held on trust for the Group and that they are not the private property of the individuals appointed as trustees. This can be done by inserting the Group's bank account number after the names of the trustees and it will facilitate the recovery of tax by the Group.

*Addition to Sub–Rule 28 xi. See page 137.

Rule 28 xii   Motor Vehicles, Vessels and Aircraft

(a) The Group Treasurer must ensure that motor vehicles, vessels and aircraft owned by the Group are properly registered, licensed and insured as necessary and that all requirements as to their condition and testing or any other matters are fulfilled.

(b) Motor vehicles must be registered either in the name of the Group or in the name of a nominee, in which case the registration must show that the person is a nominee of the Group and not the private owner of the vehicle.

Rule 28 xiii   Equipment

The Group Treasurer must maintain proper inventories of all equipment owned by the Group, including furniture, training equipment, musical instruments or equipment of any other kind.

Rule 29 — Safe Custody of Documents

Rule 29 i

The Group Secretary must ensure that documents relating to the ownership of property and equipment and all other legal and official documents, together with any documents of historical importance or interest are kept in a safe place, namely a fireproof safe or strongroom. Such documents may be safeguarded by using the Association's Headquarters Deeds Custody Service.

Specific documents that must be safeguarded in this way are:

- Declarations of Trust.
- Title Deeds to land or buildings.
- Registration documents issued by the Association.
- Stock and Share Certificates.
- Documents relating to motor vehicles, vessels and aircraft.
- Insurance policies.
- Documents relating to registration under the Charities Act, 1960 or equivalent, and to exemption from taxation or exemption or relief from the General Rate.

Rule 29 ii

The Group Secretary must keep a register of such documents, with details of their location.

Rule 30 — Insurance

*Complete Rule amended. See page 137.

Rule 30 i

Every Scout Group must maintain adequate insurance cover, to be reviewed annually, in respect of the following risks:

- property and equipment, including effects in

transit, at camp or on expeditions;

- motor vehicles, including passenger risk, in the United Kingdom or abroad;
- marine and boating risks;
- aircraft and air travel risks;
- equipment and personal injury risks in respect of any activity not covered by insurance effected by the Association's Headquarters.

Note: The Association's Headquarters provides for the following insurance cover:

1. The Scout Association Indemnity Policy

This policy covers Scouters and other persons authorised by the Association to be in charge of Cub Scouts, Scouts or Venture Scouts in the United Kingdom against claims by third parties alleging legal liability arising out of accidents or incidents occuring during any authorised Scouting activity. It extends to cover those in charge of Cub Scouts, Scouts or Venture Scouts while they are engaged in properly organised Scouting activities anywhere on the Continent of Europe as well as British Scouters who assume temporary responsibility, and other persons temporarily charged with responsibility, for parties of foreign Scouts who visit the United Kingdom to participate in Scouting activities organised by a British home unit.

The Scout Association Indemnity Policy does not cover liability arising out of the ownership or driving of motor vehicles, or injuries to third parties or damage to third party property arising out of the ownership or operation of boats. The Association's Headquarters can arrange for such insurance cover and will provide details of available facilities on application.

2. The Personal Accident and Medical Expenses Policy

This policy covers all Members of the Association in England, Wales and Northern Ireland while they are in the United Kingdom or on

71

authorised visits within the Continent of Europe. In Scotland, a similar policy is provided, details of which can be obtained from Scottish Headquarters.

Parties of up to five foreign Scouts visiting the United Kingdom to take part in official Scouting activities organised by a British home unit are also covered by this policy. Larger parties must be insured by the host unit. This can be done through the appropriate Headquarters as defined above and it may be necessary for an additional premium to be paid.

Rule 30 ii

In order for the insurance cover provided by Headquarters to be effective, the rules of the Association must be complied with, particularly those rules governing the organisation of activities and safety precautions applying to activities (*See Rule II, 76 viii*).

Rule 30 iii   Indemnities

If a Group is arranging to use land, premises or any facilities belonging to another organisation or individual and is required to sign an agreement which includes an indemnity clause or a requirement for special insurance cover, details must be sent to the Association's Headquarters as soon as possible and before proceeding with the arrangements. The risks involved may already be covered or, if they are not, cover must be arranged, either through the Association's Headquarters or otherwise, before an indemnity is given.

Rule 30 iv   Injuries and Fatalities

(a) If any person, whether a Member of the Association or not, suffers personal injury or dies in the course of, or arising out of, a Scouting activity or while on, or in connection with, any Scout unit property, the Association's

Headquarters must be informed immediately. On receipt of this information, the Association's Headquarters will issue the necessary instructions and forms in respect of possible claims under the Indemnity or Accident Insurance Policies.

(b) In the event of an injury or fatality, no admission of responsibility must be made unless advised by the Association's Headquarters.

Rule 31   Disputes within the Scout Group

Rule 31 i

The following procedures are to be used only if informal efforts to resolve disputes have been made and have failed. They do not apply to the suspension of members of the Group, which is covered by *Rules 3 x* and *5 v above*.

(a) Disputes arising between the Scouters of a Group and the Group Executive Committee or the Group Council and disputes between the Group Executive Committee and the Group Council must be referred to the District Commissioner and the District Executive Committee. In the case of a Sponsored Group, the Sponsoring Authority must be consulted.

(b) The same procedure as in *Rule 31 i (a) above,* must be followed in the event of a dispute between the Executive Committee of a Venture Scout Unit and the Group Executive Committee.

(c) In the event of a dispute between the Sponsoring Authority of a Sponsored Group and the Group Scout Leader, Group Executive Committee or Group Council, the matter must be referred to the District Commissioner and the District Executive Committee. Both or all the parties in the dispute must be given reasonable opportunity to state their case *(See Rule 4 ii (e) above, Rules I, 52 and I, 71).*

The Scout District

Rule 32

The purpose of the Scout District within the structure of The Scout Association is to provide leadership, advice and support for Scout Groups and local Venture Scout Units in an area whose boundaries will correspond, in so far as is possible, with those of local authorities. National Headquarters, in consultation with County and District Commissioners, decides where these boundaries are to be drawn, guided by the principle that the District Commissioner should be able to be in touch with all the Groups and all the Members of the Association in the area and bearing in mind the local boundaries established by The Girl Guides Association. On occasion, it may be necessary to adapt boundaries to suit these various needs.

Rule 33

Registration of Scout Districts

Rule 33 i

Scout Districts are registered by the Association's Headquarters at its discretion on the recommendation of the County Commissioner.

Rule 33 ii

Application for registration must be made on Form A which must be completed and signed by the prospective District Secretary and District Commissioner. The form is sent to the Association's Headquarters through the County Secretary, who must sign it to signify the approval of the County Commissioner and forward it through the National Headquarters.

Rule 33 iii   Annual Registration of Scout Districts

Annual Registration must be effected by the Scout District and Form DR, the District Annual Registration Summary must be completed *(see also Rule I, 45)*.

Rule 33 iv   Suspension of District Registration

(a) The County Commissioner may suspend any Scout District, pending consideration by the Association's Headquarters of a recommendation for the cancellation of its registration.

(b) During any suspension as in *Rule 33 iv (a) above,* all the functions of the District will cease and, except as the Association's Headquarters may otherwise direct, all Commissioners, Scouters, Instructors, Administrators and Advisers and the holders of all other appointments in all Groups in the District are automatically suspended.

(c) The County Executive Committee must provide for the administration of the property and finances of a District and of the Groups within the District during any suspension *(See also Rule 5 v above)*.

Rule 33 v   Cancellation of District Registration

The Association's Headquarters may cancel the registration of a Scout District and withdraw all Warrants held in the District on the recommendation of the County Commissioner, acting in consultation with the District Commissioner and the District Chairman.

Rule 34 Composition of the Scout District

The Scout District is led by the District Commissioner, who is supported by:

□ Assistant District Commissioners, District Scouters, Administrators and Advisers;
□ The District Scout Council;
□ The District Executive Committee.

Rule 35 The Appointment of Commissioners and Scouters in the Scout District

Rule 35 i   The District Commissioner

(a) Recommendation for the appointment of a District Commissioner is made on Form LC, after enquiries as in *Rule 10 i above* have been made by the authority making the recommendation. A prospective District Commissioner may not commence his duties until this procedure has been completed.

(b) The Association's Headquarters will issue a Warrant on acceptance of the recommendation and this will be presented in an Investiture by the County Commissioner as soon as possible after receipt.

(c) The Warrant of a District Commissioner remains valid until 31st March in the fifth year following the year of its issue. The appointment may then be renewed at the discretion of the County Commissioner, provided that the training obligations of the appointment, as in *Rule I, 35 i (d)* have been met.

(d) District Commissioners – Leader Training Obligations

Within three years of appointment, a District Commissioner must complete the appropriate Basic Training. He must complete the appropriate Advanced Training within five years of appointment or of completing Basic Training, whichever is the later.

(e) Ceasing to Hold the Appointment of District Commissioner

On ceasing to hold the appointment of District Commissioner, the Commissioner must surrender his Warrant to the County Secretary for cancellation. If the service of the Commissioner has been satisfactory, the County Secretary will return the cancelled Warrant and complete Form X, which he will send to the Association's Headquarters. If the service has not been satisfactory, the cancelled Warrant will be sent with the Form X to the Association's Headquarters.

Rule 35 ii   Assistant District Commissioners

(a) The procedure for the appointment of Assistant District Commissioners and for the issue of their Warrants is as for District Commissioners in *Rule 35 i (a)* to *(d) above.*

(b) The Warrants of Assistant District Commissioners

The District Commissioner must specify the responsibilities of an Assistant District Commissioner *(See Rule I, 36 ii)* by completing and signing his Warrant, informing the District Secretary of the details of the appointment so that he may complete the District records.

(c) Port Commissioners

Port Commissioners may be appointed as Assistant District Commissioners in appropriate Districts for the purpose of supervising the

Association's interests, particularly in respect of travel and of the membership of Deep Sea Scouts.

(d) Ceasing to hold the appointment of Assistant District Commissioner.

On ceasing to hold appointment as an Assistant District Commissioner, the holder must surrender his Warrant to the District Secretary, who will forward it, together with a completed Form X to the County Secretary for cancellation. If the service has been satisfactory, the County Secretary will return the cancelled Warrant to the former holder and complete Form X and send it to the Association's Headquarters. If the service has not been satisfactory, the cancelled Warrant will be sent with the Form X to the Association's Headquarters.

Rule 35 iii   The Appointment of District Scouters

(a) District Scouters, namely the District Cub Scout Leader, the District Scout Leader and the District Venture Scout Leader, are appointed in exactly the same way as Scouters in the Group *(See Rule 10 above)*. Their appointments are subject to the same conditions as those of Group Scouters.

(b) All District Scouters are required to complete Advanced Training within five years of appointment or of completing Basic Training, whichever is the later.

Rule 36   Qualifications and Responsibilities of District Appointments

Rule 36 i   The District Commissioner

(a) Age Limits

The minimum age limit for appointment as a District Commissioner is a matter of the discretion of the County Commissioner and the Association's Headquarters. The maximum age limit is sixty-five.

(b) Responsibilities

The District Commissioner is responsible to the County Commissioner and to Headquarters for:

□ the maintenance of the Association's policy in the District and for encouraging and facilitating the training of Members of the Association as appropriate throughout the District;

□ visiting Scout Groups and local Venture Scout Units and advising their leaders how to conduct them in accordance with the Association's policy as defined in these rules and in the Association's handbooks;

□ encouraging the formation and operation of the District Scout Council, the District Scout Fellowship, if so decided in accordance with *Rule I, 51 i,* Scout Groups and local Venture Scout Units and assisting in their effective working;

□ securing the harmonious co-operation of all Members of the Association in the District and settling any disputes between them (*See Rules 31 above* and *I, 71*);

- performing all duties specified in these rules for District Commissioners in respect of training and administration, particularly duties in respect of appointments, registrations, Membership of the Association, decorations and awards (*See Rule II, 54*), the achievement of minimum standards for Scout Groups and Sections within Groups (*See Rule 7 above*);
- the observance of all rules related to the conduct of Scouting activities particularly to camping and activities requiring the observance of safety precautions (*See Rule II, 71–81 inc.*);
- the supervision of all Cub Scouts, Scouts and Venture Scouts and all Scouters visiting the District and the reporting of any special circumstances or incidents to the County Commissioner;
- co-operation and the maintenance of good relations with members of The Girl Guides Association and other youth organisations in the District and ensuring that the Association is adequately represented on local committees particularly youth committees.

(c) In respect of the District Scout Council and the District Executive Committee the District Commissioner must nominate the District Chairman and certain members of the committee (*See Rules I, 38 iii and I, 40 i*).

(d) The District Commissioner represents the District on the County Scout Council, together with the District Chairman and a Scouter from a Group in the District.

(e) The District Commissioner is an ex officio member of all Councils and Committees and their sub-committees within the District.

(f) If the office of District Commissioner is vacant, the County Commissioner will either nominate an Assistant District Commissioner or another Commissioner to act in this capacity or will perform these duties himself.

Rule 36 ii   Assistant District Commissioners

(a) Age Limits
The age limits for appointments as an Assistant District Commissioner are as for District Commissioners (*See Rule 36 i above*).

(b) Assistant District Commissioners are appointed to assist the District Commissioner with general or particular duties (e.g. General Duties, Cub Scouts, Scouts, Venture Scouts, Leader Training, District Scout Fellowship). The District Commissioner will specify the nature of the individual's duties by completing the appropriate section of the Warrant.

(c) Responsibility for Leader Training
The Assistant District Commissioner (Leader Training) must be an experienced Scouter and must have completed Advanced Training. His functions are:

□ to assist the District Commissioner with the training of leaders and particularly with the initial training of newly appointed leaders;

□ to arrange for the training of Scouters in the District.

Rule 36 iii   District Scouters

(a) Age Limits
The age limits for appointment as a District Scouter are:
Minimum: District Cub Scout Leader and District Scout Leader – twenty, District Venture Scout Leader – twenty one. Maximum: sixty-five.

(b) District Scouters are appointed to fulfil certain functions in relation to the Sections of Scouting, e.g. District Cub Scout Leader. The duties of such appointments will be defined by the District Commissioner at the time of appointment.

Rule 37

The District Scout Council

Rule 37 i

The District Scout Council is the electoral body which supports Scouting in the District. Under the chairmanship of the District Chairman, it must hold an Annual General Meeting in May or as soon as possible thereafter each year to:

- approve the Annual Report of the District Executive Committee, including the audited accounts;
- approve the District Commissioner's nomination of the District Chairman;
- elect a District Secretary and a District Treasurer, unless either or both are employed by the District Executive Committee in accordance with *Rule I, 40 vi;*
- elect certain members of the District Executive Committee as defined in *Rule I, 38 iii;*
- elect one Group Scouter to represent the District on the County Scout Council.

Rule 37 ii   Membership of the District Scout Council

The following are members of the District Scout Council:

- Commissioners, Scouters, Administrators, Instructors (excluding Cub Scout Instructors) and Advisers in Scout Groups and in the District and the Chairmen of Venture Scout Units in the District;
- Members and Associate Members of the Association registered in the District, including members of the District Scout Fellowship;
- persons elected or re-elected annually by the District Scout Council on the recommendation of the District Commissioner and the District Executive Committee.

(See also Rules I, 58 i (b) and I, 63 ii (c))

Rule 38 The District Executive Committee

Rule 38 i

The District Executive Committee exists to support the District Commissioner in meeting his responsibilities and to provide support for Scout Groups in the District. It is specifically responsible for:

- promoting the well-being of the Association in the District and arranging for harmonious co-operation with other organisations;
- acting in conjunction with the District Commissioner in all matters related to District finance and property;
- appointing, in consultation with the District Commissioner, a District Appointments Sub-Committee and a Chairman of such a Sub-Committee and any other sub-committees and their chairmen as the Committee may require;
- supervising the administration of Groups, particularly in relation to finance and the trusteeship of property (*See Rule 28 above*);
- attending to District administration, particularly:
- matters relating to Warrants;
- the appointment of Instructors (excluding Cub Scout Instructors), Administrators and Advisers;
- registrations, Membership of the Association, decorations and awards, examinations for proficiency badges, appointing an Assistant Secretary as Badge Secretary for the District;
- presenting an Annual Report and audited accounts to the Annual General Meeting of the District Scout Council.

Rule 38 ii   The District Appointments Sub-Committee

The functions of the District Appointments Sub-Committee are:

- to be responsible, with the District Commissioner, for interviewing applicants for Warrants and for all other appointments and satisfying themselves as to the suitability of applicants;
- considering applications for changes in Warrants in Groups or in the District.

See also Rules I, 38 iii (b) and I, 40 (i) concerning membership of the District Appointments Sub-Committee.

Rule 38 iii   Composition of the District Executive Committee

(a) The District Executive Committee consists of:

Ex officio members

The District Chairman
The District Commissioner
The District Secretary
The District Treasurer
(See also Rules I, 58 i (b) and I, 63 ii (c))

Nominated members

Persons nominated by the District Commissioner and whose membership of the Committee is confirmed at the District Annual General Meeting. They need not be members of the District Scout Council and their number may not exceed that of the elected members.

Elected members

Persons elected at the District Annual General Meeting. These should normally be four to six in number but the actual number must be the subject of a resolution by the District Scout Council and must be approved by the County

Executive Committee.

Co-opted members

Persons co-opted annually by the District Executive Committee.

The number of co-opted members may not exceed the number of members who may be elected.

(b) Sub-Committee Membership

Sub-Committees of the District Executive Committee consist of members nominated by the Committee. The District Commissioner and the District Chairman are ex officio members of all sub-committees. The District Chairman may be the Chairman of the District Appointments Sub-Committee and the Assistant District Commissioner (Leader Training) must be an invited member of the same Sub-Committee.

Rule 39 Conduct of Meetings in the Scout District

Rule 17 above as applied to meetings of the Group Council and the Group Executive Committee applies in the same way to meetings of the District Scout Council and the District Executive Committee.

Rule 40 The Appointment and Role of Administrators and Advisers in the Scout District

Rule 40 i The District Chairman

(a) The District Chairman is nominated by the District Commissioner and his appointment is approved by the District Scout Council at its Annual General Meeting.

(b) The duties of the District Chairman are:

- to work closely with the District Commissioner to encourage the well-being and progress of Scouting in the District;
- to act as Chairman at meetings of the District Scout Council and the District Executive Committee;
- to maintain close liaison with Group Chairmen throughout the District and to promote the organisation and effective working of their Group Councils.

The District Chairman may be the Chairman of the District Appointments Sub-Committee (*See Rule 38 iii (b) above*) and is an ex officio member of all Committees and sub-committees in the District.

Rule 40 ii The District Secretary

(a) The District Secretary may *either*:

be elected by the District Scout Council at its Annual General Meeting,

or:

may be employed by the District Executive

Committee, who will appoint him in consultation with the District Commissioner in accordance with *Rule I, 40 vi.*

(b) The duties of the District Secretary are:

□ to act as Secretary of the District Scout Council and the District Executive Committee;

□ to co-ordinate the work of sub-committees of the District Executive Committee;

□ to distribute to all Groups and others concerned information and instructions from Headquarters, the County and the District;

□ to maintain an up-to-date list of appointments and of the names and addresses of all Members and Associate Members as appropriate or necessary in the District;

□ to perform all other duties specified for District Secretaries in these rules.

(c) The office of District Secretary may not be combined with that of District Treasurer and may not be held by a Scouter.

(d) The Association's Headquarters must be informed of changes in the appointment and address of District Secretaries.

Rule 40 iii   The District Treasurer

(a) The District Treasurer may *either:*

be elected by the District Scout Council at its Annual General Meeting,

or:

may be employed by the District Executive Committee, who will appoint him in consultation with the District Commissioner in accordance with *Rule I, 40 vi.*

(b) The duties of the District Treasurer are:

□ to advise the District Executive Committee on all matters affecting financial control and expenditure and to prepare an annual budget;

□ to receive all monies on behalf of the District Executive Committee and the District Commissioner and to keep account of all funds and to pay out money upon authorisation as specified by the District Executive Committee;

☐ to invest any accumulated funds in accordance with *Rule 28 xi above,* as applied to Scout Districts, after consultation with the District Executive Committee or any subcommittee appointed for the purpose;

☐ to consult the County Treasurer and Group Treasurers in the co-ordination of fund raising activities;

☐ to perform all other duties specified for District Treasurers in these rules.

(c) The office of District Treasurer may not be combined with that of District Secretary and may not be held by a Scouter.

Rule 40 iv   Other District Administrators

Other administrators may be appointed by the District Executive Committee in consultation with the District Commissioner as required.

Rule 40 v   Enquiry

The appointment of all District Administrators is subject to the satisfactory completion of the enquiry procedure as in *Rule 10 i above.*

Rule 40 vi   Employment and Salaries

District Administrators may be employed and paid a salary out of District Funds at the discretion of the District Commissioner and the District Executive Committee. The Association's Headquarters must be consulted with regard to pension scheme facilities, conditions of employment, taxation and National Insurance requirements.

Rule 40 vii   District Advisers

(a) District Advisers may be appointed by the

District Executive Committee or Appointments Sub-Committee with the approval of the District Commissioner.

(b) Enquiry

The appointment of District Advisers is subject to the satisfactory completion of the enquiry procedure as in *Rule 10 i above*.

(c) District Advisers may be appointed for duties in specific activity areas e.g. Activities, Public Relations.

(d) The District Secretary must keep a record of the appointment of all District Advisers.

Rule 40 viii   Termination of Appointments of District Administrators and Advisers

The termination of the appointments of District Administrators and Advisers is as for those of Group Administrators and Advisers in *Rule 18 vi above*.

Rule 41   Finance – General

Rule 41 i

Rule 20 above, as applied to Scout Groups, applies in the same way to Scout Districts, each of which is a separate educational charity under the same obligations as a Scout Group.

Rule 41 ii

A statement of accounts as described in *Rule 20 iii above* must be presented at the Annual General Meeting of the District Scout Council, duly audited by an independent and responsible person, who need not be a qualified accountant.

Rule 42 District Bank Accounts

Rule 22 above as applied to Scout Groups applies in the same way to Scout Districts.

Rule 43 District Accounts Disposal of Assets

Rule 43 i   Disposal of Assets at Amalgamation

(a) *Rule 23 i (a) above* as applied to Scout Groups applies in the same way to Scout Districts.

(b) If the Treasurer of a District newly formed as a result of amalgamation considers it necessary, he may ask the District Executive Committee to appoint an auditor to examine the statement of account prepared by the outgoing Treasurers.

Rule 43 ii   Disposal of Assets at Closure

If it is proposed to close a Scout District, the District Treasurer must prepare a statement of account as described in *Rule 20 iii above* as applied to Scout Districts, substituting for 31st March the date on which it is prepared. This statement must be sent to the National Headquarters not less than four weeks before the proposed date of closure. The Headquarters will give instructions for the discharge of liabilities and the disposal of assets and of the books of account.

Rule 44 Preservation of Books of Account

Rule 24 above applies also to Scout Districts.

Rule 45 Payment of the Membership Subscription

Each District is required to pay the annual Membership Subscription to the Association's Headquarters in respect of the number of members shown in the Annual Registration and Census Return in the following categories:

- Commissioners.
- District Scouters.
- Members and Associate Members of the Association including members of the Scout Fellowship.

Rule 46 Fund Raising in the Scout District

Rule 46 i

All fund raising in the Scout District must be conducted in accordance with the Association's policy as defined in *Rule 26 i–viii above*.

Rule 46 ii

The Scout District is expected to support itself financially through local fund raising efforts. Levies on Scout Groups in the District are permitted with the proviso that they be of a reasonable and restricted nature as defined by the District Executive Committee.

Rule 46 iii
Fund raising conducted by the Scout District must take place within the District boundaries.

Rule 46 iv   Appeals for Funds – Districts
Scout Districts may make general appeals for funds, but before any such appeal is issued, the District Treasurer must consult the County Executive Committee and his National Headquarters.

Rule 47   Grant Aid and Loans
Rule 27 above as applied to Scout Groups applies in the same way to Scout Districts.

Rule 48   Trusteeship, Property and Equipment

Rule 48 i
Rule 28 above as applied to Scout Groups applies in the same way to Scout Districts.

Rule 48 ii
Pending the disposal of the property of a Scout District which is ceasing to exist, all necessary steps must be taken by the County Executive Committee to preserve the property, assets and documents of title relating to the District.

Rule 49 — Safe Custody of Documents

Rule 29 above as applied to Scout Groups applies in the same way to Scout Districts.

Rule 50 — Insurance

Rule 50 i

Rule 30 above as applied to Scout Groups applies in the same way to Scout Districts.

Rule 50 ii

If action is to be taken in relation to effecting insurance or reporting claims, injuries or fatalities, this action must be taken by the Scouter or other adult responsible for the individual's or party's participation in the event or activity *(See Rule 30 iv above)*.

Rule 51 — The District Scout Fellowship

*Sub-Rule 51 i amended. See page 141.

Rule 51 i

The District Commissioner, in consultation with the District Executive Committee, may decide to form a District Scout Fellowship.

Rule 51 ii

The purpose of the District Scout Fellowship is to provide a body through which adults may support Scouting in the District and enjoy social activities while participating in community service.

Rule 51 iii

Membership of the District Scout Fellowship is open to any person over the age of eighteen, including those holding appointments, who will be expected to give priority to the duties of their appointments, and Venture Scouts, who will be expected to give priority to Unit activities. All members of a District Scout Fellowship become Associate Members of the Association and they may become Members of the Association if they wish to do so. They are also members of the District Scout Council and they pay the annual Membership Subscription.

★Sub-Rule
51 iv
amended.
See page 141.

Rule 51 iv
The District Commissioner may appoint an Assistant District Commissioner to lead the District Scout Fellowship.

Rule 52 Disputes in the Scout District

Rule 52 i
Rule 31 i above as applied to Scout Groups applies in the same way to Scout Districts.

Rule 52 ii
Any dispute between adult Members or Associate Members in a Scout District must be referred to the District Commissioner. If the District Commissioner is unable to resolve the dispute, or if he himself is involved in it, he must refer the matter to the County Commissioner.

Rule 52 iii
If the County Commissioner is unable to resolve the dispute, he will refer the matter to his National Headquarters for a decision which must be accepted as final by all parties.

Rule 53

The Scout Borough, the Scout Division and Appointments in Cities

Rule 53 i

Exceptionally, and with the specific approval of the National Headquarters, the Association's interests may be organised into Borough or Divisional areas and, in certain large cities, measures may be taken to modify the administrative structure of the Association to suit local circumstances.

Rule 53 ii

Borough, Divisional or City Commissioners may be appointed for liaison duties with Local Education Authorities and with local government in such areas.

The Scout County

Rule 54

The purpose of the Scout County within the structure of The Scout Association is to provide leadership, advice and support for Scout Districts and, through them, for Scout Groups in an area whose boundaries correspond, in so far as is possible, with those of local authorities. The boundaries of a Scout County are defined by the National Headquarters in consultation with the County Commissioner, bearing in mind the local boundaries established by The Girl Guides Association.

Rule 55

The Registration of Scout Counties

The registration and the cancellation of the registration of Scout Counties are matters for the discretion of National Headquarters, who may convene such committees or groups as may be necessary to make recommendations on such matters, including the amalgamation of Counties and changes in their boundaries.

Rule 56

The Composition of the Scout County

The Scout County is led by the County Commissioner, who is supported by:
☐ Assistant County Commissioners, County Administrators and Advisers;
☐ The County Scout Council;
☐ The County Executive Committee.

Rule 57 The Appointment of Commissioners in the Scout County

Rule 57 i   The County Commissioner

County Commissioners are appointed by the Headquarters of the Association in accordance with the Bye Laws of the Association.

Rule 57 ii   Assistant County Commissioners

The appointment of Assistant County Commissioners is made and is subject to conditions as specified for District Commissioners in *Rule 35 i above.*

Rule 58 Qualifications and Responsibilities of County Appointments

Rule 58 i   The County Commissioner

(a) The County Commissioner is responsible to the Chief Scout and the Association's Headquarters for maintaining the policy of the Association in the County and encouraging and facilitating the training of Members of the Association as appropriate in the County. His responsibilities include:

□ promoting the organisation and effective

working of the County Scout Council;

- □ acting with the County Executive Committee in all matters relating to finance and property and to the appointment of County Administrators;
- □ securing the services of persons suitable for appointment as Commissioners and taking such administrative measures as may be necessary concerning their Warrants;
- □ promoting the effective working of Scout Districts within the County and taking such administrative measures as may be necessary concerning the registration of Scout Districts and the receipt of the Annual Reports and audited accounts, including schedules of property, from Scout Districts within the County;
- □ performing all other duties specified in these rules for County Commissioners, particularly:
- – making recommendations for the conferring of the title *Honorary Scouter* on Commissioners giving up their Warrants (*See Rule 3 iv above*) and for the conferring of decorations and awards (*See Rule II, 54–60*);
- – arranging for the performance of the duties of District Commissioners in the event of vacancies;
- – giving decisions and, where so provided, reporting to Headquarters as appropriate on all matters referred to him, particularly disputes between District Commissioners and District Scout Councils (*See Rule 52 above*) or any other dispute (*See Rule 52 above* and *Rule I, 71*); (*See also Rule 3 x* and *Rule 5 v above* concerning Committees of Inquiry);
- – attending, if he so desires, meetings of the Committee of the Council of the Association in accordance with *Rule I, 78 ii*;
- – co-operating with all bodies whose work is relevant to Scouting and ensuring that the

Association's interests are represented to local authority youth committees.

(b) The County Commissioner is an ex officio member of all Committees and sub-committees in the County and may attend any or all meetings of all Councils and Executive Committees within the County or may nominate a representative to attend on his behalf.

(c) If the office of County Commissioner is vacant, his duties will be performed by the Association's Headquarters or by a person appointed by that Headquarters for that temporary purpose.

Rule 58 ii   Deputy County Commissioners

Deputy County Commissioners may be appointed by the Association's Headquarters on the recommendation of the County Commissioner to assist and deputise for him. The duties of such appointments will be defined by the County Commissioner at the time of appointment.

Rule 58 iii   Assistant County Commissioners

(a) Assistant County Commissioners are appointed by the same procedure as applies to the appointment of District Commissioners as described in *Rule 35 i above*. They assist the County Commissioner generally or with specific duties, viz:

Activities	Public Relations
Air Activities	Relationships
Cub Scouts	Scout Fellowship
Development	Scouts
Extension Activities	Venture Scouts
International	Water Activities
Leader Training	

(b) Assistant County Commissioners (Leader Training) must be experienced Scouters who must be qualified Leader Trainers.

Rule 58 iv   Leader Trainers and Assistant Leader Trainers

(a) Leader Trainers and Assistant Leader Trainers are appointed by the same procedure as applies to District Commissioners as described in *Rule 35 i above*. They assist the County Commissioner in providing facilities for and in encouraging the training of leaders and in organising Basic and Advanced Training as required in the County and its Districts.

(b) Before being appointed as an Assistant Leader Trainer, a Scouter must have:
□ completed Advanced Training;
□ had experience of helping on courses;
□ attended a National Trainers' Course.

(c) Before being appointed as a Leader Trainer, an Assistant Leader Trainer must have:
□ had at least two years experience in his appointment;
□ assisted on at least two Advanced Courses;
□ attended an International Training the Team Course.

Rule 59   Field Commissioners

Rule 59 i

Field Commissioners are appointed by the Association's Headquarters and assigned to work in Scout Counties to assist County Commissioners in the development of Scouting.

Rule 59 ii   Fleet Commissioners

Fleet Commissioners are appointed by and are responsible to the Association's Headquarters for duties specified at the time of their appointment.

Rule 60 The County Scout Council

Rule 60 i

The County Scout Council exists to:

- encourage the development of Scouting in the County;
- appoint, in consultation with the County Commissioner, a County Secretary and a County Treasurer, unless either or both are employed by the County Executive Committee in accordance with *Rule I, 63 viii*;
- elect members of the County Executive Committee as specified in *Rule I, 61 ii*;
- elect representatives of the County Scout Council to serve as nominated members on the Council of the Association (*See Rule I, 82*);
- hold an Annual General Meeting and to send a copy of its Annual Report and audited accounts, approved at that meeting, to the Chief Commissioner and to the Association's Headquarters.

Rule 60 ii   Membership of the County Scout Council

The County Scout Council consists of:

Ex officio members

The County Chairman.

The County President and Vice Presidents (*See Rule I, 63 i*)

The Chief Commissioner (*See Rule I, 75 i (b)*)

The County Commissioner

The County Secretary

The County Treasurer

Assistant County Commissioners

Leader Trainers

County Advisers

District Commissioners

District Chairmen or their nominees.

Invited member
The Field Commissioner.

Nominated members
Persons nominated annually by the County Commissioner in consultation with the County Chairman.

One nominated Group Scouter to represent each District Scout Council.

Co-opted members
The County Scout Council may co-opt members annually, subject to the provisions of *Rule I, 60 iii*. Such co-opted members may include representatives of organisations with whom it is desired to maintain co-operation, e.g. The Girl Guides Association, religious bodies, youth organisations and Local Education Authorities.

Rule 60 iii

The number of nominated and co-opted members may not exceed the number of ex officio members and District Scout Council representatives taken together.

Rule 61

The County Executive Committee

Rule 61 i

The County Executive Committee exists to:

- act as an Executive Committee for the County Scout Council in the development of Scouting in the County and to arrange for harmonious co-operation between Scout Districts and between units of the Association and other organisations;

- act with the County Commissioner in all matters relating to finance and property in the County;

- appoint annually such sub-committees as may be necessary for its effective working;
- present an Annual Report to the Annual General Meeting of the County Scout Council together with a statement of account duly audited by an independent and responsible person who need not be a qualified accountant.

Rule 61 ii   Membership of the County Executive Committee

The County Executive Committee consists of:

Ex officio members

The County Chairman.

The County Commissioner

The County Secretary

The County Treasurer

The Chief Commissioner *(See Rule I, 75 i (b))*.

Invited member

The Field Commissioner

Nominated members

Persons nominated annually by the County Commissioner in consultation with the County Chairman.

Elected members

Persons elected annually by the County Scout Council, of whom at least one half must be Warrant holders.

Co-opted members

Persons co-opted annually by the County Executive Committee.

Rule 61 iii

The number of nominated members and co-opted members may not exceed the number of ex officio members and elected members taken together.

Rule 62   Conduct of Meetings in the Scout County

Rule 17 above as applied to meetings of the Group Council and the Group Executive Committee applies in the same way to meetings of the County Scout Council and the County Executive Committee.

Rule 63   The Appointment and Role of Administrators and Advisers in the Scout County

Rule 63 i   The County President and Vice Presidents

County Presidents and Vice Presidents are appointed by the Association's Headquarters in consultation with the County Commissioner to encourage the well-being of Scouting in the County.

Rule 63 ii   The County Chairman

(a) The County Chairman is nominated by the County Commissioner in consultation with the County President and the National Headquarters and the nomination is approved by the County Scout Council at its Annual General Meeting.

(b) The duties of the County Chairman are:

- to collaborate with the County Commissioner in encouraging the well-being and progress of Scouting in the County;
- to act as Chairman of the County Scout Council and of the County Executive Committee and to promote their effective working;
- to maintain contact with all District Chairmen in the County and to promote and encourage the effective working of their Councils.

(c) The County Chairman is an ex officio member of all Committees and sub-committees in the County and may attend any or all meetings of Executive Committees and Councils or may nominate a representative to attend on his behalf.

(d) The Association's Headquarters must be informed of changes in the appointment of County Chairmen and their addresses.

Rule 63 iii The County Secretary

(a) The County Secretary may *either:*
be appointed by the County Scout Council in consultation with the County Commissioner, *or*:
be employed by the County Executive Committee in accordance with *Rule I, 63 vii.*

(b) The duties of the County Secretary are:
- to act as Secretary of the County Scout Council and the County Executive Committee;
- to co-ordinate the work of sub-committees of the County Executive Committee and to distribute to all concerned information or instructions from Headquarters and the County Scout Council and Executive Committee;
- to perform all other duties specified for County Secretaries in these rules.

(c) The office of County Secretary may not be combined with that of County Treasurer.

(d) The Association's Headquarters must be informed of changes in the appointment of County Secretaries and their addresses.

Rule 63 iv   The County Treasurer

(a) The County Treasurer may *either:*
be appointed by the County Scout Council in consultation with the County Commissioner, *or:*
be employed by the County Executive Committee in accordance with *Rule I, 63 vii.*

(b) The duties of the County Treasurer are:

☐ to advise the County Executive Committee on all matters affecting financial control and expenditure and to draw up an annual budget;

☐ to receive all monies on behalf of the County Scout Council, the County Executive Committee and the County Commissioner and to keep account of all funds and to pay out money upon authorisation as specified by the County Executive Committee;

☐ if the County Executive Committee so decides, to set up and maintain a County Finance and Fund Raising Sub-Committee in consultation with the County Executive Committee and to invest accumulated funds, in accordance with *Rule 28 xi above,* in consultation with such a sub-committee if established;

*Addition to Sub-Rule 63 iv (b). See page 141.

☐ to co-ordinate fund raising efforts with District and Group Treasurers;

☐ to perform all other duties specified in these rules for County Treasurers.

(c) The office of County Treasurer may not be combined with that of County Secretary.

(d) The Association's Headquarters must be informed of changes in the appointment of County Treasurers and their addresses.

Rule 63 v   Other County Administrators

Other Administrators may be appointed by the County Executive Committee in consultation with the County Commissioner.

Rule 63 vi   Enquiry

The appointment of all County Administrators is subject to the satisfactory completion of the enquiry procedure as in *Rule 10 i above.*

Rule 63 vii   Employment and Salaries of County Administrators

Rule 40 vi above as applied to Scout Districts applies in the same way to Scout Counties.

Rule 63 viii   County Advisers

★Sub-Rule 63 viii (a) amended. See page 143.

(a) The appointment of the following Advisers is made by the Association's Headquarters on receipt of an application on Form LA; a Certificate of Appointment is issued:

Activities	International
Air Activities	Public Relations
Chaplain	Relationships
Development	Scout Fellowship
Extension Activities	Water Activities

(b) Other County Advisers may be appointed by the County Executive Committee with the approval of the County Commissioner.

(c) Enquiry

The appointment of all County Advisers is subject to the satisfactory completion of the enquiry procedure as in *Rule 10 i above.*

Rule 63 ix   Termination of Appointments of County Administrators and Advisers

(a) The appointments of County Administrators and Advisers may be terminated in the same way as those of Group and District Administrators and Advisers in accordance with *Rule 18 vi above*.

(b) When a County Adviser ceases to hold his appointment, the County Secretary must complete Form W and forward it, with the cancelled Certificate of Appointment if appropriate, to the Association's Headquarters.

Rule 64

Finance – General

Rules 41 to 44 above as applied to Scout Districts apply in the same way to Scout Counties.

Rule 65

Payment of the Membership Subscription

Scout Counties are required to pay to the Association's Headquarters the annual Membership Subscription in respect of the number of members shown in the annual Census Return in the following categories:

□ Commissioners
□ Leader Trainers and Assistant Leader Trainers
□ Advisers appointed by Headquarters *(See Rule 63 viii (a) above)*.

Rule 66

Fund Raising in the Scout County

Rule 66 i
All fund raising conducted in the Scout County must be in accordance with the policy of the Association as defined in *Rule 26 i–viii above*.

Rule 66 ii

The Scout County is expected to support itself financially through its own fund raising efforts. Levies on Scout Districts and Scout Groups are permitted with the proviso that they be of a reasonable and restricted nature as defined by the County Executive Committee.

Rule 66 iii

Fund raising conducted in the Scout County must take place within the boundaries of the Scout County.

Rule 66 iv   Appeals for Funds

Before any general appeal is issued, the County Treasurer must consult National Headquarters.

Rule 67   Grant Aid and Loans

Rule 27 above as applied to Scout Groups applies in the same way to Scout Counties.

Rule 68   Trusteeship, Property and Equipment

Rule 68 i

Rule 28 above as applied to Scout Groups applies in the same way to Scout Counties.

Rule 68 ii

Pending the disposal of the property of a Scout County which is ceasing to exist, all necessary steps will be taken by the Association's Headquarters to preserve the property, assets and documents of title relating to the County.

Rule 69   Safe Custody of Documents

Rule 29 above as applied to Scout Groups applies in the same way to Scout Counties.

Rule 70   Insurance

Rule 30 above as applied to Scout Groups and *Rule 50 above* as applied to Scout Districts apply in the same way to Scout Counties.

Rule 71   Disputes in the Scout County

Rule 71 i

Rule 31 i as applied to Scout Groups applies in the same way to Scout Counties.

Rule 71 ii

Any dispute between adult Members or Associate Members of the Association in a Scout County must be referred to the County Commissioner unless it can be dealt with by the District Commissioner under *Rule 52 above*. If the County Commissioner is unable to resolve the dispute, or if he is himself involved in it, he must refer the matter to his National Headquarters for a decision which must be accepted as final by all parties.

Rule 71 iii

In the event of a dispute arising between adult Members or Associate Members of the Association in Districts in different Counties, the County Commissioner of each County must refer the matter to his National Headquarters for a decision which must be accepted as final by all parties.

National

Rule 72

The Chief Scout and Deputy Chief Scouts

Rule 72 i

(a) The Chief Scout is appointed by the Council of the Association in accordance with the Bye Laws of the Association.

(b) The Chief Scout is the Chairman of the Council of the Association.

Rule 72 ii

A Deputy Chief Scout or Deputy Chief Scouts may be appointed on the recommendation of the Chief Scout by the Council of the Association at its discretion.

Rule 73

Chief Scout's Commissioners

Chief Scout's Commissioners are appointed by the Association's Headquarters upon the nomination of the Chief Scout.

Rule 74

Headquarters Commissioners and Assistant Headquarters Commissioners

Rule 74 i

Headquarters Commissioners are appointed by the Association's Headquarters to undertake special responsibilities within the training programme.

Rule 74 ii

Assistant Headquarters Commissioners may be appointed by the Association's Headquarters to assist Headquarters Commissioners.

Rule 75

Chief Commissioners and National Councils

Rule 75 i

(a) The Committee of the Council of the Association appoints persons to be Chief Commissioners of England, Northern Ireland, Scotland and Wales at its discretion and for such periods and with such authority as it may specify.

(b) Chief Commissioners are ex officio members of all County Scout Councils and Executive Committees throughout the countries in which they are appointed.

Rule 75 ii

(a) The National Councils of each country exist to:

- advise the Chief Commissioner in all matters relating to the exercise of his discretionary powers as specified by the Committee of the Council;
- perform such administrative and executive duties as may be delegated to them by the Committee of the Council, which may include the management of their financial affairs.

(b) The Committee of the Council of the Association makes and approves constitutions for National Councils in order to facilitate the performance of delegated duties.

Rule 76 The Chief Executive Commissioner

Rule 76 i

(a) The Committee of the Council appoints at its discretion a Chief Executive Commissioner to be responsible for:

- the co-ordination of all the work of the Headquarters of the Association at its various establishments;
- the implementation of the policy of the Committee of the Council;
- the financial control of Headquarters;
- the Field Commissioner service;
- such special tasks as may be requested by the Committee of the Council.

(b) The Chief Executive Commissioner is an ex officio member of the Council of the Association and of its Committee.

Rule 76 ii Deputy Chief Executive Commissioner

(a) The Committee of the Council may appoint at its discretion a Deputy Chief Executive Commissioner to assist and deputise for the Chief Executive Commissioner.

(b) A Deputy Chief Executive Commissioner appointed under *Rule 76 ii (a) above* is an invited member of the Committee of the Council.

Rule 77 The Headquarters of The Scout Association

The Committee of the Council of the Association maintains a Headquarters with a departmental structure as required for the implementation of its policy and to provide services and materials necessary for the proper conduct and development of Scouting.

Rule 78 The Committee of the Council of the Association

Rule 78 i

The Committee of the Council of the Association exists to manage the business of the Association in accordance with the Bye Laws of the Association.

Rule 78 ii Composition of the Committee of the Council

The Committee of the Council consists of:

Ex officio members

The Chief Scout

The Deputy Chief Scout(s)
The Treasurer of the Association
The Chief Executive Commissioner
The Chief Commissioners of England, Northern Ireland, Scotland and Wales
The Headquarters Commonwealth Commissioner

Elected members

Ten other members of the Council of the Association, elected at its Annual General Meeting.

Co-opted members

Up to five other members of the Council of the Association, co-opted subsequent to the Annual General Meeting in any year.

Rule 78 iii   Rights of Attendance at Meetings of the Committee of the Council

Headquarters Commissioners, County Commissioners and Commissioners representing Overseas Branches of the Association *(See Rule I, 83)* have the right of attendance at meetings of the Committee of the Council and may put forward matters for discussion without vote on giving a fortnight's notice to the Secretary of the Committee.

Rule 79   Sub-Committees of the Committee of the Council

Rule 79 i

The Committee of the Council delegates certain of its powers to three Sub-Committees:
The Programme and Training Sub-Committee
The Finance Sub-Committee
The General Purposes Sub-Committee

Rule 79 ii

The membership and terms of reference of these Sub-Committees is determined by the Committee of the Council but two or more members of the Committee must serve on each. Other persons may become members of the Sub-Committees provided that the majority of the members of any Sub-Committee are members of the Council of the Association.

Rule 80

National Boards

Rule 80 i

The Programme and Training Sub-Committee is advised by National Boards appointed from time to time with the approval of the Committee of the Council to consider aspects of the Association's training programme, viz:

The National Cub Scout Board
The National Scout Board
The National Venture Scout Board
The National Activities Board
The National Leader Training Board

Rule 80 ii

The membership and terms of reference of these Boards is determined by the Committee of the Council.

Rule 81

Headquarters Boards

Rule 81 i

The Finance Sub-Committee is advised by the following Headquarters Boards, appointed from time to time with the approval of the Committee of the Council to consider aspects of administration related to finance, viz:

The Scout Shops Limited Board

The Scout and Guide Trust Fund Management
Committee
The Baden-Powell House Board

Rule 81 ii

The General Purposes Sub-Committee is
advised by the following Headquarters Boards
appointed from time to time with the approval
of the Committee of the Council to consider
specific aspects of administration, viz:
The Publications Board
The Religious Advisory Board
The Roland House Board
The Camp Sites Board
The Awards Board
The Scout Association Trust Corporation
Board

Rule 81 iii

The membership and terms of reference of all
Headquarters Boards is determined by the
Committee of the Council.

Rule 82 The Council of The Scout Association

Rule 82 i

The Scout Association is governed by a Council of between 300 and 500 members as determined by the Royal Charters of 1912 and the
Supplemental Royal Charters of 1949, 1959 and
1967.

Rule 82 ii Composition of the Council of the Association

The Council consists of:
Ex officio members
The President of the Association

The Chief Scout
The Deputy Chief Scout(s)
The Treasurer of the Association
The Chief Executive Commissioner
Headquarters Commissioners
The Chairmen of National Boards
The Chief Commissioners of England, Northern Ireland, Scotland and Wales
The Chief Commissioners of Overseas Branches *(See Rule I, 83)*
The County and Area Commissioners of the United Kingdom

Nominated members

Each County Scout Council in the United Kingdom and each Overseas Branch nominates one or more representatives on the basis of one for every 10,000 members declared by the County or Branch at the time of the annual census taken prior to the nomination. Once nominated, these representatives serve for three years unless another representative is nominated in their place. They may be salaried officials of County Scout Councils but may not be salaried officials of Headquarters.

Elected members

Up to sixty other persons of whom not more than three may be full-time employees of the Association, elected at the Annual General Meeting of the Council. Elected members serve for three years.

Overseas

Rule 83 — The Overseas Branches of the Association

Rule 83 i

Branches of the Association are established in certain territories within the Commonwealth, with local Chief Scouts and Chief Commissioners.

Rule 83 ii

A model form of Constitution for Overseas Branches may be obtained from the Association's Headquarters. Any Constitution granted by the Association's Headquarters may be withdrawn at its discretion.

Rule 83 iii

Variations in the rules of the Association may be sanctioned by the Association's Headquarters to suit the local circumstances of an Overseas Branch.

Rule 83 iv

The Headquarters Commonwealth Commissioner is an ex officio member of all Scout Councils and their Executive Committees in Overseas Branches. At his discretion, he may appoint a representative to attend meetings of such Councils or Executive Committees and to vote on his behalf. He is responsible to the Committee of the Council for the efficiency and well-being of Scouting in Overseas Branches and for relations with Scout Associations in Commonwealth countries.

Rule 83 v

Changes in the office of Secretary of an Overseas Branch must be notified to the Association's Headquarters by the new office holder as soon as possible after appointment.

Rule 84

The World Organisation

Rule 84 i

The Scout Association is the only Scout Organisation in the United Kingdom recognised by the World Scout Conference and registered with the World Scout Bureau.

Rule 84 ii   The International Fellowship of Former Scouts and Guides

(a) The United Kingdom is a member country of the International Fellowship of Former Scouts and Guides.

(b) Members of a District Scout Fellowship who are or become Members of the Association *(See Rules 3 and 51 above)* are automatically members of the International Fellowship of Former Scouts and Guides.

General

Rule 85 — Associate Organisations

Rule 85 i

The Scout Association has approved the establishment of the following organisations whose aims and purposes relate to those of the Association:

The Scout and Guide Graduate Association *(See Rule I, 85 ii);*

The Student Scout and Guide Organisation *(See Rule I, 85 iii);*

Student Scout and Guide Clubs *(See Rule I, 85 iv);*

The International Scout and Guide Club *(See Rule I, 85 v).*

Rule 85 ii   The Scout and Guide Graduate Association

(a) The Scout Association and The Girl Guides Association have approved the constitution and rules of The Scout and Guide Graduate Association, which include the provision that its Committee shall maintain close liaison with the Headquarters of both Associations in order to keep its policy in line with the aims and practices of the two Associations.

(b) The Scout and Guide Graduate Association exists to:

□ render to the Scout and Guide Movement such services as may accord with the Association's special abilities;

□ promote Scout and Guide co-operation;

□ support and encourage university and other similar Scout and Guide Clubs.

Rule 85 iii   The Student Scout and Guide Organisation

The Student Scout and Guide Organisation exists to:

- provide a forum for discussion about matters that affect all Student Scout and Guide Clubs and their members and to act as a channel of communication between the Headquarters of The Scout and Girl Guides Associations and the Student Scout and Guide Clubs;
- assist and encourage emergent Student Scout and Guide Clubs;
- ensure the continuance of rallies open to all students;
- co-operate with the Scout and Guide Graduate Association;
- co-ordinate United Kingdom participation in international Student Scout and Guide events;
- assist and co-ordinate the work of member Clubs *(See Rule I, 85 iv).*

Rule 85 iv   Student Scout and Guide Clubs

(a) A Student Scout and Guide Club exists to:

- provide a social framework within which friends may exchange ideas informally and maintain and renew or acquire an interest in the principles of Scouting and Guiding;
- render service as a club to Scouting and Guiding and to the community at large;
- utilise the special training of its members in critical appraisal and discussion of all aspects of the Movement and, by research, to develop a sensitivity to new ideas in the field of youth work and the presentation of suggestions to help towards improving the quality and effectiveness of the Movement;
- create a wider understanding of and sympathy with the work of the Movement, particularly among fellow students by the

spreading of information and by example;
- □ encourage among students an interest in all spheres of youth work in alliance with other organisations.

(b) Student Scout and Guide Clubs are recognised and given Associate status when approval is given by the Student Scout and Guide Organisation to their constitution and rules and when the Headquarters of The Scout and Girl Guides Associations are advised that this approval has been given.

(c) Amendments to the constitution and rules of a Student Scout and Guide Club may only be made with the approval of the Student Scout and Guide Organisation in consultation with the Headquarters of The Scout and Girl Guides Associations.

Rule 85 v The International Scout and Guide Club

(a) The International Scout and Guide Club is a club for present and former members of the Scout and Guide Movements of any nationality and is run and governed by its members. All its members are expected to comply with the primary condition of membership which is that of continuance of their existing loyalties within the Movements.

(b) The aims of the Club are:
- □ to promote personal international friendships, a wider knowledge of the world-wide Scout and Guide Movements and a better appreciation of other people and other lands;
- □ to provide a centre where Scouts and Scouters and Guides and Guiders from other countries can make friendly contact with Scouting in London and obtain up to date information on both Movements throughout the world.

(c) The Club's constitution and rules have received the approval of the Headquarters of The Scout and Girl Guides Associations. Any amendments to the constitution must have similar joint approval.

Note: Information about the International Scout and Guide Club may be obtained from the Headquarters of either The Scout Association or The Girl Guides Association.

*New sub-Rule 85 vi. See page 146.

Rule 86

Companies Associated with The Scout Association

Rule 86 i   Scout Shops Limited

Scout Shops Limited, the service for the supply of the material requirements of the Association, is a company owned by the Association and the entire profit from its trading is covenanted to the Association. The Board of the company is a Headquarters Board *(See Rule 81 i above)*.

Rule 86 ii   The Scout Association Trust Corporation

(a) The Scout Association Trust Corporation is a limited company auxiliary to The Scout Association. Its powers and constitution are stated in its Memorandum and Articles of Association and it is licensed as a trust corporation by the Lord Chancellor.

(b) The Scout Association Trust Corporation may act as sole trustee for land and investments for The Scout Association and for Scout Councils of Groups, Districts and Counties in the United Kingdom, excepting Scotland. It is also a trustee for the Scout and Guide Trust Fund, which is a common investment scheme for The

Scout and Girl Guides Associations, authorised by the Secretary of State for Education and Science under Section 22 of the Charities Act, 1960.

Rule 87

Conduct

The conduct of Members of the Association must be such as to maintain the reputation of the Association.

Rule 88

Political Activities

Rule 88 i

The Scout Movement is not connected with any political body. Members of the Association in uniform, or acting as representatives of the Association, must not take part in any party political meetings or activities.

The Association, being concerned to help young people prepare for and take a constructive place in society, encourages, through its training programme, the development of a positive attitude to the needs of the community. It is accepted that, from time to time, this will involve members of the Movement with current social issues, some of which are controversial and may therefore have a political dimension.

In pursuance of the Association's Aim, each invested member of the Movement shall, within the bounds of his age and mental maturity, be encouraged:

□ to involve himself in the processes by which decisions are made within the Association and, to that end, to understand the organisation of the Association;

□ to become more aware of major social issues at local, national and international level;

□ to understand the processes of decision making by organisations and by government, and to become aware of the individual's role in such processes.

Rule 88 ii

If a recognised public authority makes a public request for volunteers to take action to avoid grave public danger or inconvenience, whether it arises from an industrial dispute or not, a Group Scout Leader or the Leader of a local Venture Scout Unit, in both cases with the consent of the District Commissioner, may offer the services of Scouts or Venture Scouts, provided that each individual participates entirely voluntarily.

Rule 89 Expression of Opinions on the Association's Policy

Members of the Association may not express opinions on matters of policy or on any matter if it will appear that they are speaking or contributing on behalf of the Association when appearing on television, speaking on radio or writing for or being interviewed by the Press, unless they have previously obtained permission to do so from the Association's Headquarters.

Rule 90 Standards of Premises and Equipment

All premises, sites, vessels, aircraft, vehicles and

other equipment in general public view or likely to be seen by the public must be maintained to a standard likely to reflect credit upon the Association.

Rule 91 Protected Badges, Designations, Trade Marks and Copyright

Rule 91 i

The following badges and all Scout designations are protected and may not be used, nor may permission be given for their use, without the prior permission of the Association's Headquarters:

Badges and Emblems

The World Membership Badge;

The Arrowhead Badge and all badges, the design of which incorporates the Arrowhead Badge;

The Armorial Bearings of The Scout Association;

The Silver Wolf.

Designations

The name of the Association;

All designations of Members and appointments which incorporate the word 'Scout';

The title 'Scouter'.

Rule 91 ii Authority for Reproduction of Protected Badges and Designations

(a) Scout Executive Committees may, under the authority of this rule, authorise reproduction of:

The Arrowhead Badge,
The name of the Association;
All badges of the Association (excluding the
World Membership Badge and the Armorial
Bearings of the Association),
on the following items:

> flags, letterheads, forms, reports and other
> stationery, band instruments, signs and
> notice boards, publicity material, pictures of
> events or places connected with Scouting and
> on fund raising items.

(b) The use of badges and designations permitted in *Rule 91 ii (a) above* is restricted to the item being commissioned. Permission may not be given to any manufacturer or printer to produce any range of items incorporating badges or designations without additional prior permission from the Association's Headquarters.

Rule 91 iii   Trade Marks

Trade Marks of which the Association is the proprietor or registered user are subject to protection and may not be used without the prior written permission of the Association's Headquarters.

Rule 91 iv   Approval by the Association

No organisation or individual may state or imply that any item has been approved, in content, quality or otherwise, by the Association without the prior written permission of the Association's Headquarters.

Rule 91 v   Copyright

No organisation or individual may reproduce any substantial part of any publication, including these rules, the copyright of which is vested in the Association, without the prior written permission of the Association's Headquarters. The Executive Committees of Scout Groups,

Districts and Counties may authorise the reproduction of extracts of limited length suitable to meet a specific purpose in the production of material required to further their work.

Rule 91 vi   Assignment of Copyright

The copyright of works which is vested in the Association may only be assigned by the Association's Headquarters.

Rule 92   Correspondence

Members of the Association may not address correspondence on matters related to Scouting or as representatives of the Association to any Royal personage, Department of State, Embassy or Legation at home or abroad, to any Scout Association Headquarters abroad or to the World Scout Bureau, Committee or Conference except after consultation with and through the Association's Headquarters.

Rule 93   Hitch-hiking

Members of the Association engaged on Scouting activities must not travel by hitch-hiking, except in cases of genuine emergency.

Rule 94   Marching

Parties of Scouts when marching must have responsible traffic pickets at the head and the rear. At night, such pickets must show a white light at the head and a red light at the rear.

Appendix A
Agreement between a Group Executive Committee and Sponsoring Authority as to Ownership of Funds and Other Property

NOTE: The following letter is merely a specimen and need not be followed exactly. In particular, the division of the Group bank account into two equal halves is put forward only as an example.

Date..............

Dear Group Secretary (or Dear Sponsoring Authority),

This letter is written in accordance with *Policy, Organisation and Rules* of The Scout Association, to confirm the following agreement which we have made together.

1. That the following items are the property of the ....Group of The Scout Association:

(i) The Headquarters of the Group, being a moveable wooden hut at present situated at...........

(ii) The tents and other camping equipment of the Group, an inventory of which is annexed to the Trust Deed of the Group dated..... day of ....19.....

(iii) (Specify here any other items which it is agreed belong to the Group).

2. That the following items are the property of the Sponsoring Authority:

(Specify here any items which it is agreed belong to the Sponsoring Authority).

★Clause 3 amended. See page 141.

3. In the event of the Group being disbanded one half of the balance of the Group's account at the (.......... Branch of ....Bank) (National Savings Bank, Account Number ....) shall belong to the Sponsoring Authority and one half to the Group.

Yours faithfully,

Appendix B

Agreement between a District Commissioner and a Sponsoring Authority

I.......... (full name) ....of
..............(address) ....as
........(description of Office held relating to
the Sponsorship) agree to undertake the Sponsorship of the ....(title of Scout Group)
..........Group of The Scout Association
(hereinafter referred to as 'the Group') and I
further acknowledge that such Sponsorship
shall be subject to the following conditions:

1. I accept without reservation the policy of
The Scout Association as set out in *Policy,
Organisation and Rules* in force at the date hereof
(hereinafter referred to as '*P.O.R.*').

2. I understand the requirements as to
minimum standards set out in *P.O.R.* and that
these must be applied to the Group.

3. The *Sponsoring Authority/*Group Executive Committee/*District Executive Committee shall be responsible for the provision of a
suitable Headquarters for the Group.

4. *Membership of the Group is open to any
person who may become a member of The
Scout Association as laid down in *P.O.R.*
*Membership of the Group is restricted as follows:

(insert wording as required)

*The Sponsoring Authority shall nominate
those persons who are to hold Warrants in the
Group in consultation with the Group Scout
Leader and the District Commissioner.

5. *The Sponsoring Authority shall actively
assist the Group Scout Leader and the District
Commissioner in ensuring the continuity of
leadership within the Group.

6. *The Sponsoring Authority shall be responsible for the financial support of the Group.

*The Sponsoring Authority has agreed with the Group Executive Committee the following fund-raising policy:

(insert wording as required)

7. I undertake to enter into an agreement with the Group Executive Committee or their Trustees determining the ownership of freehold and leasehold property; equipment and furniture; and investments and funds as between the Sponsoring Authority and the Group and to countersign a statement of such determination or allocation to be lodged annually with the District Scout Council.

8. I undertake to give the G.S.L. the fullest possible encouragement and support in carrying out his work and in the development of Scouting in the Group as described in *P.O.R.* and other official publications of The Scout Association.

9. I understand that this Agreement shall be subject to review and revision as necessary five years from the date hereof or at such earlier date as may be agreed between myself and the District Commissioner then in office.

Date . . . .

Sponsoring Authority

I acknowledge that the above is a true statement of the Agreement reached, after due consultation, between . . . .(name of Sponsoring Authority) . . . . .and myself for the conduct of Scouting in the . . . .(title of Group) . . . . .Group.

Date . . . .

District Commissioner

*NOTE: *Delete as required.*

Amendments

The following replaces Rule 3 ii (which appears on page 12):

Rule 3 ii Rights and Conditions of Membership

Members of the Association may:
□ wear the approved uniform of the Association;
□ wear the World Membership Badge.
Adult Members who do not hold appointments will receive the appropriate Membership Card on payment of the annual Membership Subscription.

Rules 3 viii, ix and x (which appear on pages 14 and 15) are to be renumbered as Rules 3 xi, xii and xiv, and replaced by the following:

Rule 3 viii Student Membership of the Association – Qualifications

Students in full time Higher Education (e.g. at a University or a College of Education) may become Student Members of the Association by making the Scout Promise.

Rule 3 ix Rights and Conditions of Student Membership

Student Members of the Association may:
□ wear the approved uniform of the Association;
□ wear the World Membership Badge;
□ receive the appropriate Membership Card.
A Student Member is not required to pay the annual Membership Subscription, except that any full time student who is a Venture Scout. holds a Leader Warrant or registers as a Member of The Scout Association in accor-

Amendments

dance with *Rule 3 iv above* will be required to pay the Membership Subscription.

Rule 3 x   Acquisition of Student Membership

Student Membership is acquired by registration with the District Secretary of the District in which the student is in full time Higher Education.

The following is added to Rule 3 (which appears on pages 12 to 17):

Rule 3 xiii   Termination of Student Membership

Student Membership of the Association may be terminated:

□ in accordance with *Rule 3 xi (a) above*;
□ by ceasing to be a student in full time Higher Education.

The following replaces Rule 10 iv (b) (which appears on page 39):

(b) The renewal of Warrants is subject to the satisfactory completion of Leader Training appropriate to the appointment as follows:

□ Group Scout Leaders and Section Leaders must complete the appropriate Basic Training within twelve months of appointment and the appropriate Advanced Training within five years of appointment.
□ A Scouter who is not a Section Leader must complete the appropriate Basic Training within twelve months of appointment.

Amendments

The following is added to Rule 22 iii (which appears on page 58):

Group funds may be invested in special schemes organised by their Scout County, which have been approved by the Committee of the Council *(See Rule I, 28 xi (d))*.

The following replaces Rule 28 ii (a) (which appears on page 65):

(a) All freehold and leasehold land and premises, buildings used under formal licence, investments and endowment funds must be held by trustees appointed as specified in *Rule I, 28 ii (b)*.

The following replaces Rule 28 ii (c) (which appears on page 66):

(c) Trust Deeds must be prepared in accordance with the Association's model Declaration of Trust, details of which will be sent by the Association's Headquarters to the Group's solicitors.

The following replaces Rule 28 ii (d) (which appears on page 66):

(d) If exceptional circumstances appear to make it necessary or desirable that property be held upon trusts other than those laid down in the appropriate Trust Deed, the matter should be referred to the Association's Headquarters.

Amendments

The following replaces Rule 28 x (which appears on page 68):

Rule 28 x   Joint Occupation of Premises by Scout and Girl Guide Units

A special Declaration of Trust, which must provide for the formation of a joint management committee, must be drawn up if premises are to be owned and occupied jointly by Scout and Girl Guide units. This does not apply if the premises are used jointly under licence or if the premises are occupied by other similar arrangements. A copy of the appropriate Declaration of Trust will be sent by the Association's Headquarters to the solicitors acting for the Scout and Girl Guide units.

The following is added to Rule 28 xi (which appears on page 69):

(d) Group Treasurers may assume that they have specifically designated powers if they invest Group funds in schemes which have the approval of the Committee of the Council.

The following replaces Rule 30 (which appears on pages 70 to 73):

Rule 30   Accidents and Insurance

Rule 30 i   Accidents

If any person, whether a Member of the Association or not, suffers personal injury (where injury necessitates treatment by a doctor, dentist or at hospital) or dies in the course of, or arising out of, a Scout activity or while

Amendments

on, or in connection with any Scout property; or if an accident during a Scout activity results in damage to third party property, Headquarters must be informed immediately. On receipt of this information the Association's Headquarters will issue the necessary instructions and forms in respect of possible insurance claims. In the event of an injury or fatality, or damage to third party property, no admission of liability must be made unless advised by the Association's Headquarters.

Rule 30 ii   Insurance Cover

Every Scout Group must maintain adequate insurance cover, to be reviewed annually, in respect of the following risks:

- property and equipment, including the risk of loss or damage to equipment whilst in transit or at camp or on expeditions;
- motor vehicles, including passenger risk, in the British Isles or abroad;
- marine and boating risks;
- aviation and air activity risks;
- authorised Scout visits abroad.

Note: The Association's Headquarters can arrange insurance cover in respect of all the above.

Rule 30 iii   Personal Accident and Medical Expenses

This insurance is provided by Headquarters and covers the total Membership, up to the maximum age of 70 years, as shown on the Annual Census Returns together with new Members joining during the year, in the British Isles except Scotland, but including British Scouts in Western Europe. Details of the current benefits under this policy may be obtained from Headquarters. Special travel insurance should be obtained for authorised Scout visits abroad. In

Amendments

Scotland a similar policy is provided, details of which can be obtained from Scottish Headquarters. Parties of up to five foreign Scouts visiting the British Isles to take part in Scout activities organised by a British home unit are also covered by this policy. Larger parties can be insured by the host unit if the visiting Scouts are not already insured through their home Association. This can be arranged through the appropriate Headquarters as defined above on payment of additional premium.

Supplementary insurance cover can be arranged through Headquarters to provide higher benefits for Leaders. Supporters are not provided with the same automatic basic Personal Accident Insurance as Members. They can be insured under the basic policy and can have the benefit of Supplementary Insurance similar to that which is available to Leaders.

Rule 30 iv   The Scout Association Legal Liability Policy

This policy provides cover for Commissioners, Scouters and other persons authorised to be in charge of or assist with Scout activities, against claims made by Members under their control, or their parents/guardians, or by third parties, alleging legal liability arising out of accidents or incidents occuring during any authorised Scout activity. It extends to those authorised to be in charge of Cub Scouts, Scouts or Venture Scouts while they are engaged in properly organised and authorised activities abroad, as well as British Scouters who assume temporary responsibility for parties of foreign Scouts visiting the British Isles to participate in Scout

Amendments

activities organised by a British home unit.

The policy also extends to protect those responsible for the organisation and running of Scout fund raising events and covers the property owner's liability which rests upon any Scout authority which owns or is responsible for land and/or buildings (except for liability under any agreement – see *Rule I, 30 v*).

The Scout Association Legal Liability Policy does *not* cover legal liability arising out of the ownership and/or driving/or piloting of motor vehicles, aircraft and/or gliders. Nor does it fully cover liability for injuries to third parties and/or damage to third party property arising out of the ownership or operation of boats. The Association's Headquarters can arrange marine liability insurance and will provide details on application.

Rule 30 v   Indemnities

If a Scout Group is arranging to use land, premises or other facility belonging to another authority, organisation or an individual, and is required to sign an agreement or indemnity, details must be sent to the Association's Headquarters as soon as possible. The acceptability of the agreement or indemnity terms and the adequacy of the Association's Legal Liability Policy in relation to them must be confirmed before proceeding with the arrangements or signing an agreement or indemnity.

Rule 30 vi

For the insurance cover by Headquarters to be effective, the Rules of the Association must be complied with, particularly those Rules governing the organisation of activities and safety precautions applying to activities (*See Rules II, 71–76 inc.*).

Amendments

The following replaces Rule 51 i (which appears on page 94):

Rule 51 i

The District Commissioner, in consultation with the District Executive Committee, should form a District Scout Fellowship.

The following replaces Rule 51 iv (which appears on page 95):

Rule 51 iv

The District Commissioner may appoint an Assistant District Commissioner (Scout Fellowship) who will be responsible for maintaining effective liaison between the District Commissioner and the District Scout Fellowship.

The following is added to Rule 63 iv (b) (which appears on page 107):

☐ to ensure that if the County is running an Investment Service for Group funds, the rules of the scheme have the approval of the Committee of the Council.

The following replaces Clause 3 of Appendix A (which appears on page 131):

3. In the event of the Group being disbanded one half of the balance of the Group's account at the (. . . . . Branch of . . . . Bank) (National Savings Bank, Account Number . . . .) shall belong to the Sponsoring Authority and one half shall be deemed to be assets of the Group to be disposed of in accordance with *Rule 23 ii above.*

Amendments

The following replaces Rule 4 ii (a) (which appears on page 19):

(a) The organisation which sponsors the Group shall appoint a person or committee to act as the Sponsoring Authority. The District Commissioner must be informed of the appointment.

The following is added to Rule 4 ii (b) (which appears on page 20):

☐ in the case of a religious body, to support the Group Scouters in their responsibilities for spiritual development within the training programme of the Cub Scouts, Scouts and Venture Scouts.

The following replaces Rule 4 v (c) (which appears on page 22):

(c) The agreement must be reviewed by both parties at least every five years but may be reviewed at any time at the request of either party. It must also be reviewed in the event of a change of Sponsoring Authority or Group Scout Leader.

Amendments

The following replaces Rule 13 v (b) (which appears on page 46):

(b) Responsibilities

The Scout Leader is responsible in conjunction with the Patrol Leaders' Council for the training of Scouts, subject to the general supervision of the Group Scout Leader and with the assistance of Assistant Scout Leaders and Instructors.

The following replaces Rule 13 vii (b) (which appears on page 46):

(b) Responsibilities

The Venture Scout Leader is responsible in conjunction with the Unit Executive Committee for the training of Venture Scouts, subject to the general supervision of the Group Scout Leader if the Unit is part of a Group or of the District Commissioner if it is a local Venture Scout Unit. He may be assisted by Assistant Venture Scout Leaders and Instructors.

The following replaces Rule 63 viii (a) (which appears on page 108):

(a) The appointment of the following Advisers is made by the Association's Headquarters on receipt of an application on Form LA; a Certificate of Appointment is issued:

Activities
Air Activities
Chaplain
Development
Duke of Edinburgh's
   Award Scheme
Handicapped
International
Mountain Activities
Public Relations
Relationships
Scout Fellowship
Water Activities

Amendments

The following is added to Rule 7 (which appears on pages 28 to 33):

Rule 7 v   The Beaver Colony

The Beaver Colony is made up of a maximum of twenty-four Beavers.

The following replaces Rule 11 i (which appears on page 41):

Rule 11 i

Instructors, other than Beaver, Cub Scout and Occasional Instructors, are appointed and re-tired by the Group Scout Leader subject to the approval of the District Commissioner and the District Appointments Sub-Committee. The appointment must be reviewed every five years and may be renewed.

The following replaces Rule 11 ii (which appears on page 41):

Rule 11 ii   Beaver and Cub Scout Instructors

(a) Beaver and Cub Scout Instructors are appointed and retired by the Beaver Leader or the Cub Scout Leader as appropriate with the approval of:
□ the Venture Scout Leader, in the case of Venture Scouts;
□ the Guider and the Scout District Commissioner concerned, in the case of Ranger Guides;
□ the District Commissioner and the Group Scout Leader, in the case of others.
(b) Cub Scout Instructors should attend a Cub Scout Instructors' Course as soon as possible after appointment.

Amendments

Rules 13 ii and iii (which appear on pages 44 and 45) are to be renumbered as Rules 13 iv and v and replaced by the following:

Rule 13 ii   The Beaver Leader
(a) Age Limits
The age limits for the appointment of Beaver Leaders are:

Minimum: twenty

Maximum: sixty-five

(b) Responsibilities
The Beaver Leader is responsible for the programme of a Beaver Colony, subject to the general supervision of the Group Scout Leader and with the assistance of Assistant Beaver Leaders, Instructors and Beaver Instructors.

Rule 13 iii   Assistant Beaver Leaders
(a) Age Limits
The age limits for the appointment of Assistant Beaver Leaders are:

Minimum: eighteen

Maximum: sixty-five

(b) Responsibilities
The responsibilities of Assistant Beaver Leaders are specified by the Beaver Leader, who should have regard to the desirability of developing the Assistant's leadership potential.

The following replaces Rule 25 i (which appears on page 60):

Rule 25 i
In order to meet the costs of Headquarters services and the costs of organising and administering the Association nationally and to provide for meeting the Association's obliga-

Amendments

tions to World Scouting, every Scout Group and local Venture Scout Unit is required to pay each year the Membership Subscription, the amount of which is decided by the Committee of the Council of the Association, in respect of Membership of the Group or Unit who are shown on the Annual Registration and Census Return in the following categories:

□ Cub Scouts
□ Scouts
□ Venture Scouts
□ Scouters
□ Instructors, Beaver Instructors and Cub Scout Instructors (excluding Occasional Instructors)

The following is added to Rule 25 (which appears on pages 60 to 61):

Rule 25 iv   Beavers – Affiliation Fee

A Beaver Colony will pay an Affiliation Fee each year, the amount of which is decided by the Committee of the Council of the Association.

The following is added to Rule 85 (which appears on pages 122 to 125):

Rule 85 vi   Beavers

Beavers exist to provide a programme of activities within the framework of Scouting for boys between the ages of six and eight years. A Colony may be formed only within a registered Scout Group with the approval of the District Commissioner, after consultation with the District Executive Committee and the Sponsoring Authority, if appropriate. Beavers are not

Amendments

Members of The Scout Association but Beaver Leaders, Assistant Beaver Leaders and Beaver Instructors are appointed in accordance with *Rules 10, 11 and 13 above*. Beaver Colonies pay an annual Affiliation Fee. Full details are set out in the pamphlet *Beavers: Guidelines for Provision*.

Amendments

Amendments

Amendments

Amendments

Amendments

Amendments

Directory

173

N.B. *Passim* as used in this Directory denotes references throughout both Volumes which are too numerous to detail individually.

Special Terms

Headquarters

Within the organisation of Scouting in the United Kingdom, there are headquarters pertaining to Scout Groups. Districts, Counties and also National Headquarters in Scotland and Northern Ireland and the Headquarters of the Association, in London, with offices also at Gilwell and Lancing.

It will be clear from the wording of each rule which headquarters is being referred to; references to 'the Headquarters' or 'his Headquarters' appear in sub-sections of rules and refer to previous definitions which will be found in the same rule.

Section

The Sections of a Scout Group are:
The Cub Scout Pack
The Scout Troop
The Venture Scout Unit

Unit and Group

The word 'Unit', spelled with a capital letter, invariably refers to a Venture Scout Unit. A 'Scout unit' is any registered Scouting formation. Similarly, 'Group', with a capital, invariably means a Registered Scout Group, while 'group' means only 'a number of'.

Scouts

In previous versions of *P.O.R.*, it has been the practice to abreviate 'Cub Scouts, Scouts and Venture Scouts' to *Scouts,* written in italics. This has often led to the misinterpretation of rules and the full form has been used throughout this edition, favouring total clarification over brevity.